WORKSHOPS
AND
SEMINARS

WORKSHOPS AND SEMINARS

PLANNING, PRODUCING, and PROFITING

by
Pat Roessle Materka

A SPECTRUM BOOK

PRENTICE-HALL, INC.
Englewood Cliffs, New Jersey 07632

Library of Congress Cataloging-in-Publication Data

Materka, Pat Roessle.
Workshops and seminars.

Bibliography: p.
Includes index.
1. Seminars—Handbooks, manuals, etc. I. Title.
AS6.M37   1986   658.4'56   85-28296

ISBN 0-13-967787-9

A SPECTRUM BOOK

Printed in the United States of America

This book is dedicated to my parents,
Ernstine and Rudolph B. Roessle,
who instilled in me the values of high goals,
positive thinking,
and life-long learning.

CONTENTS

ACKNOWLEDGMENTS   xi
PREFACE   xiii

Chapter 1: The Learning Explosion   1

Adult education is happening everywhere, in classrooms, boardrooms, kitchens and gyms, as 20 million Americans pursue professional advancement and general life enrichment.

Chapter 2: What's In You for This?   9

You say you have no formal teaching training? Don't discount your other credentials, like talent, enthusiasm, and "real world" experience.

Chapter 3: What's In It for You?   16

Workshop leaders report that teaching adults brings them professional recognition, social contact, and psychic rewards. Some of them also make lots of money.

Chapter 4: What's In It for Them?   27

What motivates adult learners? What distinguishes them from shorter and younger species of students? A guide to common physical and psychological characteristics.

Chapter 5: Researching and Designing Your Program 34

It's like mixing a salad. You need a combination of lecture, small group activities, exercises, and open discussion to create a well paced, varied learning experience.

Chapter 6: Facilitating Discussions 46

Asking the right questions is more important than knowing all the answers.

Chapter 7: Getting Participants Involved 52

A long-winded lecture is often the least effective teaching method. In this learning-by-doing workshop, Dean N. Osterman demonstrates how you can become a better teacher by turning the floor over to the students.

Chapter 8: Places, Spaces, Props, and Plugs 58

Group involvement can be enhanced or inhibited by seating arrangements and visual aids. Circles work better than columns. And skip the slides if you can say it with newsprint.

Chapter 9: Getting Off to the Right Start 73

Be organized, be personable, but above all, be early.

Chapter 10: Quitting While You're Ahead 78

Always leave the group wishing for more. Then they'll invite you back.

Chapter 11: Evaluations 81

Solicit both praise and criticism, and get it in writing!

Chapter 12: Bombs Away! 90

Sure-fire ways to bore, annoy or alienate your audience—from trainers who have survived these experiences.

Chapter 13: Dealing with Problem Participants 97

You meet the nicest people in workshops . . . but there are exceptions. Introducing the monopolizer, the interrupter, the rambler, the arguer and other nonconformists.

Chapter 14: Conquering Stage Fright   105

You're nervous about speaking in front of a group? Join the club. Here's how to turn that panic into positive energy.

Chapter 15: Tricks of the Acting Trade   113

How can you make the 50th workshop sound as fresh as the first? Adapt the same techniques as stage performers. Actor-director Robert L. Burpee tells what to do with your hands, your voice, your face, and your feet.

Chapter 16: Promotion and Marketing   121

If nobody hears about you, nobody's going to come. Here's how to test before you invest; gain sponsorship; design a dynamic brochure; get free publicity and become a media star.

Chapter 17: Are You Ready for the Big Time?   133

Lawrence D. Kokkelenberg started out as a neighborhood social worker. He now conducts seminars for the American Management Institute as well as training sessions for corporations throughout the country. Here's how he did it.

Chapter 18: A Talk with Danny Simon   137

Even playwright Neil Simon's big brother is on the teaching circuit with his workshop on comedy writing for television.

Chapter 19: The Last Word   142

Tell them what you said.

Appendix A: Workshop Leader's Checklist   144

Appendix B: Titling Your Workshop   146

Appendix C: Workshop Evaluation   148

Appendix D: Detractor Detector   150

Appendix E: Sample Press Release   152

Appendix F: Sample Radio PSA   153

Bibliography   155

Index   161

ACKNOWLEDGMENTS

This page appears at the beginning of the book, but it was the last page to be written. Even as final chapters were coming together, I was fortunate to be receiving advice and encouragement from my family, friends, and business associates. I owe them all immense gratitude, especially:

Barbara J. Wilson, who typed the manuscript with great skill and patience;

My friends Diane Ciampa, Colleen Stafford, Marlene Konnar, and Roger Sutton, who made important contributions to the concept and content;

The professional trainers and consultants who took part in hours of interviews, including Jacqueline Allen, Charlotte Whitney, Fred Steingold, Dean Osterman, Robert Burpee, Danny Simon, Tess Kirby, Joyce Morgan, Ken Jones, Don Krebs, Sheila Feigleson, Faye Mapely, Dorothy Lemkuhl, Christine Liu, Larry Kokkelenberg, Tavi Fulkerson, Francine Surgerer, Beverly Smith, Diane Farber, Jeanne Paul, Curtis Van Voorhees, Tom Connellan, and Lila Green;

My daughter, Shannon, and my son, Marc, for keeping my spirits up and the house in order while I sat glued to the typewriter;

And especially to Bob, for always pushing me to try new things and putting up with the consequences.

PREFACE

The publication of my first book, *Time In, Time Out, Time Enough,* flung me into a career field for which I was totally unprepared. Newspaper articles appeared, portraying me as an expert on time management. Professional organizations invited me to give speeches and workshops. Local businesses approached me about conducting in-service training seminars. A planning committee asked if I would present a program for an upcoming state conference. A local community college proposed that I design a six-week course.

I was delighted. What a great way to promote the book and earn a little moonlighting income. I was flattered. Nobody had ever considered me an expert on anything before.

I was terrified.

As a writer, I had spent 10 years holed up in a quiet cubicle drafting press releases. Just me and the typewriter. Conducting an interview, I was used to letting other people do all the talking. How could I address an audience of 40 to 50 people? Nor was I a natural-born teacher. It had taken me four years to housebreak our golden retriever!

Other questions arose. How much do you charge? (How much are you worth?) How long should the presentation be? How large an audience can you handle? What about audiovisuals and handouts?

In short, what do you do after you say "yes"?

Two years and some 200 presentations later, I may not have all the answers, but I've gathered enough to give you a toehold in this uniquely rewarding business.

This book also represents the collective wisdom of several workshop leaders, trainers, speakers, and consultants whom I've interviewed. You will meet them on these pages: people who in "real life" are attorneys and accountants, homemakers and handymen, all moonlighting as instructors on everything from the practical ("How to Install Your Own Plumbing") to the fanciful ("How to Develop Your Sixth Sense").

This book will take you through the basics of:

Planning: Finding out which topics are of interest to adult learners. Organizing your subject matter into a workshop or short course format. Test marketing the program on a small scale.

Promoting: Building your professional credibility. Designing a dynamic brochure, display ad, and press release. Getting free publicity for yourself and your program.

Producing: Creating a workshop that is involving and instructive. Using audiovisuals and other aids. Handling problem participants. Evaluating your efforts.

Profiting: Beginning to market your program to a wide range of business, professional, and educational organizations. Realistically assessing the risks and rewards.

NO MONEY DOWN

You can begin with little or no financial investment. You are your own most important resource. You're also banking on your skills in a specific area of interest, your willingness to share them with others, and above all, your enthusiasm.

The risks are manageable. At worst, you may invest time and effort in a program that fails to attract an audience large enough to enable you to break even. If so, it's back to the drawing board. You can still learn from the experience.

The rewards are limitless. For starters, the field can be quite lucrative. Seasoned instructors can often command several hundred dollars per day for their services and may earn even more by mounting their own seminars or full-scale conferences. But most people are in it for the professional and psychological rewards. What other kind of work puts you so squarely in touch with others who share your values and interests? And gives you the tangible satisfaction of helping others?

It can boost your career. An investment counselor added new clients after initiating a free evening course on "Choosing Mutual Funds." The owner of a wine and cheese shop gained plenty of free advertising through his presentations on "Touring California Vineyards." An antique dealer brought new customers to his shop by giving slide lectures on period furniture and art glass.

Finally, it can add a new dimension to your life and a welcome change of pace. If you sit at a desk all day, what could be better than to kick up your heels in the evening and lead an aerobic dance class?

But, you may be saying, "I've had no training as a teacher. I haven't even had formal instruction in the field I plan to teach." Don't let that stop you. You don't need a certificate from Cordon Bleu in Paris to offer a course in brioches and croissants. You don't need to be a former Mr. Universe to conduct weight conditioning classes. Good credentials are relevant, but they are not necessarily a prerequisite.

What counts most is your content, and your own practical experience. Adult learners like to be taught by persons who have achieved success in the area they are teaching about. You can share personal insights—not just readings from somebody else's textbook.

If your program is well planned and presented, if it delivers what it promises, you will build a reputation as an expert. And that reputation will carry you forward.

I know what you're thinking. What if it bombs? What if you offer this program, and nobody shows up? What if you're booed off the podium? (Do you really think you could be booed off the podium?)

In the chapters that follow, we'll explore all the things that could go wrong (and how to prevent them). What you need now is motivation and confidence. So let me paint you a nicer scenario:

You are an outgoing, likeable person, highly competent in your profession, avocation or craft. You propose the idea of a short course or workshop in this subject area, and find there are scores of people who share your interest. Your program attracts a large audience, who seem highly appreciative of your efforts. They look upon you as an expert.

Because your name has been appearing in brochures and newspaper ads, other organizations seek out your services. You are in demand as a consultant to large corporations and as a keynote speaker for dinner meetings and conferences.

Your fame continues to spread. You agree to guest appearances with Phil Donahue and Johnny Carson. Publishers' agents hound you about writing a book. And what about audio and video tapes? Franchises? International subsidiaries?

This fantasy can take you as far as you wish. The information in this book will get you started.

A brief disclaimer: This book is not intended as a definitive survey of adult education in Western culture. It focuses on one central learning experience—the workshop—and how to make it a success.

You bring the expertise in the subject matter. I'll show you the most effective ways to share it with others—and reap many rewards in the process.

Chapter One

The Learning Explosion

Adult and continuing education: behind that somewhat stodgy, academically ponderous phrase is one of the most dynamic, rapidly expanding fields of the decade. Are you interested in investment strategies? Assertiveness training? Japanese management theories? Conversational French? If you want to learn about it, chances are someone is teaching it. And the converse may be true about your own field of expertise. If it interests you, it will probably interest plenty of others.

The field of adult education is growing so rapidly, and in so many directions, that its scope can only be estimated. William A. Draves, director of the Learning Resources Network, a national network serving organizations that provide classes to adults, reckons that more than 20,000 programs are in operation, not including those formally administered by community colleges and other higher education institutions. "Ten percent of the total U.S. population—over 20 million people—are involved in some form of non-credit learning today, and the numbers are constantly growing," Draves states.

Adult education covers a sprawling terrain. It includes: the orientation for new employees at a manufacturing plant; swim-and-trim classes at the local "Y"; a church-sponsored retreat for married couples; a travelogue presented by the public library; a hands-on demonstration of the office's new word-processing equipment.

As that variety suggests, adult education is no longer just the province of the school system. It may be offered under the auspices of a multinational corporation or a small storefront business. Professional and social organizations sponsor workshops, as do recreation centers, museums, churches, and labor unions. And while an evening math refresher course may be taught in a local high school or college classroom, the workshop on Italian pastries may be held in a restaurant kitchen; the auto maintenance and repair course takes place in a mechanic's garage.

What do these learning activities have in common?

- They have a focused objective. People enroll to learn a new skill or to feel more personally and professionally competent. Meeting new friends and having fun may be among their other incentives.

- They take place in a relatively short time—usually ranging from a one-hour, one-time workshop to a course that meets weekly over a period of 4 to 10 weeks.

- They don't carry academic credit. They may provide other forms of accreditation, such as Continuing Education Units (CEUs), which are available to participants in many professional development programs; other courses meet special certification requirements for attorneys, accountants, physicians, and other practitioners. But they don't lead to a bachelor's or graduate degree.

- They are taught by volunteer or part-time instructors who are knowledgeable about the subject matter but do not necessarily have formal training or experience as teachers.

That last point was the genesis for this book. It is intended as a practical guide for the nonexperienced teacher of short courses and workshops. But before we get into the *Who* (you and the participants) and the *How* (to put it together), here's some background on *Where* and *Why* the boom in adult education is happening.

ADULT EDUCATION—IT'S EVERYWHERE

"Historically and until very recently, adult and continuing education has been the province of three distinct agencies: educational institutions, professional associations and employers," observes Professor Lawrence S. Berlin, chairman of the graduate program in adult and continuing education at the University of Michigan and a veteran of more than 20 years in the field. He continues: "Now a fourth provider has come on the scene: the private entrepreneur, whose rapid rise to prominence has been nothing short of spectacular. The once quiet, almost sedate marketplace has become one of enormous competition for power and profit."

When you tally in that fourth category, you begin to imagine the scope of the adult education industry. It encompasses the following:

- Academic institutions
- Business and industry
- Cultural settings
- Recreation organizations
- Professional associations
- Trade unions
- Social organizations
- Independent adult learning centers

Academic institutions. Traditionally, colleges and universities have had a clearly defined niche in adult education, according to Berlin. Drawing upon academic and research resources, they served up scholarly courses in art appreciation and Shakespeare. Many colleges and universities are phasing out these types of noncredit enrichment activities, placing their sole emphasis on traditional academic degree programs and research. But community colleges continue to actively court the adult learner with practical courses in business, personal development, hobbies, and home improvement. Public schools in many communities offer a similar range of night classes, including high school equivalency coursework.

Business and industry. Companies invest billions of dollars each year enrolling their employees in various professional development seminars and bringing in consultants to conduct training programs. More and more large companies are setting up their own training departments. Once reserved for top-level executives, these educational opportunities are increasingly being extended to all levels of employees, from vice-presidents to clerical staff. Nonprofit organizations such as the Red Cross and the Girl Scouts also invest a large share of their budgets into training volunteers. And one of the largest providers of adult education of all is the U.S. government.

Cultural settings. Where can you learn about French Impressionists without enrolling in the university for credit? The art museum, of course. Many offer full schedules of courses from art appreciation to life drawing. At natural history and science museums as well, volunteer docents provide lectures and guided tours. Many libraries sponsor book review sessions and literary discussions. And if you're lucky enough to live near a planetarium, you can probably sign up for a guided tour of the solar system.

Recreation organizations. These organizations may include the local community center, a city park and recreation department, and the local YM–YWCA. Serving as family gathering places as well as activity centers, these organizations traditionally sponsor workshops more oriented toward leisure-time interests— sports and fitness, hobbies and crafts. But many are introducing programming aimed at professional development as well.

Professional associations. Whether you work in data processing or dentistry, fundraising or finance, there is an organization for you. If you are involved in a broad field such as education or sales, there are dozens for you to affiliate with. Many of these associations sponsor training programs to meet certification and licensing requirements in fields such as law, medicine, accounting, and real estate. They also hold state and national conferences. And what are conferences composed of? Lots of workshops.

Trade unions. Labor organizations provide educational programs to keep members abreast of a wide variety of issues—collective bargaining, negotiation techniques, health and safety issues, supervisory skills, labor history, and politics.

Social organizations. Whenever a group of people are gathered, sharing common goals and interests, there is also the potential for exchanging information. Examples of such social organizations are churches and fraternal groups.

Independent adult learning centers. Perhaps the most recent category to emerge on the scene is adult learning centers, organizations that act as coordinators, sponsors, or brokers for individual workshop instructors. Some are loosely affiliated with universities or public school systems; others operate independently. They tend to have names composed of words like *free, open, community, learning, exchange,* and *network.* Some examples include Network for Learning in New York City; Communiversity in Kansas City; the Class Factory in Houston; Open University in Washington, D.C.

WHY IS THIS HAPPENING?

The exploding demand for adult learning activities in all areas—professional development, practical skills, health and recreation, self-improvement—is related to a number of American demographic trends. For example, consider the following changes in the national lifestyle:

Technological change. Telephones and television revolutionized the process and speed by which we receive information, but the technological changes that have followed the advent of computers are mindboggling. Rapidly, inevitably, computers are making their way into every office, home, and school system. The technology is evolving so fast it's almost impossible to keep up with. Every time a company installs new automated equipment or upgrades its present system, it must provide training sessions for the staff who will be using it. In the public sector, there remains a steady demand for courses in "How To Buy a Home Computer," and "Beginning Programming."

But computers represent only one part of the trend. Other kinds of new technology are changing the fields of medicine, agriculture, science. New specialties and subspecialties are constantly evolving. It's partially through professional development conferences and seminars that new techniques and research findings are funneled to practitioners. Many states mandate continuing education for such professionals as pharmacists and physicians to insure their accountability and competence.

New career patterns. Technological change has made some jobs obsolete and created others. People no longer feel "locked in" to a particular career path. In several surveys of participants in adult education programs, half to two thirds say that they are enrolled "for the purpose of advancing in their careers or changing careers." Women who are returning to the workforce after a period of staying at home for childrearing make up a sizable chunk of this market.

Workers used to be labeled "unstable" if they changed employers or positions too often; now they are more likely regarded as versatile and enterprising.

Economic issues. Fluctuating unemployment, inflation, and investment trends fuel a persistent demand for courses and seminars related to personal financial planning, tax-deferred savings, or understanding the stock market. Ironically, when unemployment rates are high, adult education prospers. "When people are laid off from work they go back to school to retrain for new positions," a community college admissions officer explains.

Whether in good times or a recession, people are always interested in learning better ways of making or managing money. Courses in "How To Start Your Own Home Business" are consistently popular. Even workshops on raising bees and buying antiques appeal to the human desire to be self-sufficient and financially independent.

Educational attainment. "The more people know, the more they want to know." One of the strongest predictors of whether you will enroll in any continuing education program in the future is how much education you've had in the past.

The education level of American adults has risen dramatically in the past half-century. In 1940, only half of all adults aged 25 and older had finished elementary school. By 1967, the median years of schooling had reached grade 12, according to the U.S. Census. A 1977 Census report shows that 84 percent of all citizens between ages 20 and 24 have completed high school and/or attended college.

The vast majority of us do not look upon learning as "kid stuff" but as a lifelong endeavor.

Leisure time. The shorter work week is coming, futurists predict, as the labor force increases and factories and offices become more automated. Better educated and more affluent, Americans will have more time to explore leisure pursuits. The bets are that large numbers of us, gregarious by nature, will spend much of this time in adult learning centers—not huddled around the home video screen.

Population shifts. Finally, one reason for the boom in adult education is that there are simply more adults. The American population is getting older. The National Center for Education Statistics has projected that by the year 2000 the United States will be dominated by persons in their middle years.

The shifting age patterns have emptied some elementary schools and created a tight job market for teachers of young children. But at the opposite end of the spectrum, it's a different story! Adults are returning to school in record numbers. The baby boom generation, now in their thirties and forties, find themselves caught in the "promotion squeeze." Career ladders are crowded. There aren't enough good middle management jobs to accommodate all the ambitious candidates. Consequently, many enroll in classes in business skills to better their chances. Others accept their lack of job mobility and channel their energies into other adult learning activities such as the arts, hobbies, physical fitness, and other forms of personal enrichment.

As people live longer, they will spend more years in retirement. Persons over 65, the fastest growing segment of the population, constitute one of the largest markets for continuing education. For people of all ages, but especially the elderly, the classroom offers a safe, interactive environment for social contact and broadening horizons.

HUSTLERS AND PROFITEERS

There's another side to this rosy picture of boundless opportunity and profit. The field of adult and continuing education is growing so quickly, and in so many directions, it is highly vulnerable to the unscrupulous and the incompetent. Anyone can run an ad in the newspaper or print up a brochure, listing false credentials and misleading program content. What recourse do participants have if the program does not live up to their expectations? Like the medicine man of old, the dishonest seminar leader can blow into town, make his pitch, take your money, and run.

The situation is of genuine concern to professionals in the business like Larry Berlin, who observes:

> We have no meaningful, coherent national policy governing the provision of services.

> Extension services on many university campuses have been dismantled, due to budget cutbacks. Many of their programs have been absorbed by the independent learning centers. College professors have joined the ranks of private consultants in conducting seminars for business and industry. Recreation organizations offer workshops in career skills. With so much criss-crossing and overlapping of purposes, how do those of us in the field of adult education insure quality?

> Adult and continuing education is a multibillion dollar industry that currently has no regulatory agency—government or otherwise—to insure its integrity. Opportunity abounds, for hustlers and hucksters as well as the conscientious entrepreneur.

So you see what you're getting into: a field that is evolving, not static, and not totally immune to controversy and growing pains.

Adult education may be acclaimed the wave of the future, but it appeals to the pioneer spirit—the American drive to be self-sufficient and independent. At the base of all the reasons people enroll in classes and seminars is a desire to expand their knowledge, to understand themselves and the world a little better, and to feel more in control of their lives. Respond to these needs, and you're in for a very rewarding experience. Welcome aboard!

Chapter Two

What's in You for This?

Month after month, Martin tops his sales quota at Consolidated Gizmos. He has been asked to conduct a seminar on "Closing Techniques" at the next regional sales conference.

Frank and Janet are family therapists in private practice. They are concerned about the increase in domestic problems in their community in the aftermath of a plant closing. They decide to promote a weekend retreat on "Coping with Unemployment."

Now that her children are in school full-time, Lois has opened a home-catering business. She offers to instruct a series of gourmet cooking classes at the "Y" to help publicize her talents.

Andy is a trained auto mechanic, but his avocation is wildlife photography. Teaching an evening course in camera work will help him pay off the film-processing equipment in his basement.

The routes that bring people to the field of adult education are as varied as the subjects they teach. Each of us has different professional skills, talents, hobbies, and personal interests, and each of us has different motives for deciding to share them with others. But as teachers, many of us have one trait in common: a complete lack of preparation and experience.

IN THE CRYSTAL BALL

Growing up, we all had dreams of the careers we might enter some day: a firefighter perhaps, or a ballerina, or a pro football player, or a veterinarian. But none of us decided as small children, "Hah! When I grow up, I will conduct seminars and work-shops!"

Nor was there much in our high school or college years that prepared us for the unnerving experience of speaking in front of our peers. Not merely speaking, in fact. *Teaching.* Passing on knowledge.

Yet here you are, at this unexpected career juncture. And whether you volunteered to conduct a seminar or were talked into it, whether you are teaching for pay or for free, you want it to be a success.

The aim of this book is to help you make it a success. The aim of this chapter is to get you started.

What you need now is confidence.

You're not alone in your inexperience. The vast majority of trainers come from entirely unrelated fields. As Larry Nolan Davis points out:

> In large part, modern adult education falls outside the realm of formal educational institutions. Its practitioners, the adult educators, are largely nonacademic. Titles such as staff de-veloper, inservice trainer, training director, facilitator, and human resource developer are appearing in many organiza-tions. To varying degrees the people who work under these ti-tles have received specialized training in preparation for this work. The bulk of adult education, however, is being under-taken by men and women who have received little or no spe-cial preparation and who, having other full-time professions, do not think of themselves particularly as adult educators. They are commonly school principals, personnel directors, program chairpeople of various service and religious organi-zations, supervisors, union leaders, counselors, or simply workers in the wide variety of human organizations that make up a modern industrial society.[1]

The day you are assigned to teach five new employees how to use the office's word-processing equipment, you have entered the realm of adult education.

And only a fraction of it takes place in office settings. Adult education, as I've said, is happening in school buildings, com-munity colleges, churches, museums, hotels and conference cen-ters, recreation buildings, private homes, and swimming pools.

Thus, the credentials you need to teach depend mostly on

---

[1]Larry Nolan Davis, *Planning, Conducting and Evaluating Workshops* (Austin: Learning Concepts, Inc., 1967), p. 5.

the subject matter. If you'll be training upper-level managers on complex auditing and accounting procedures, roll out your M.B.A., C.P.A., and Ph.D. Will you teach an evening course in "Overcoming Math Anxiety" or "Conversational Spanish"? Academic credentials count when you're teaching an academic subject. But you don't need a fine arts degree to teach aerobic dancing or raku pottery. You just need to be good at it. What counts most to people taking an adult education course or workshop is real-world, practical experience. They want a teacher who has "been there."

BEING A CATALYST

Diane L. Ciampa has a degree in special education and is working toward a Ph.D. in business and psychology in "interpersonal processes." But in developing her "Different Drummer" stress management workshop she drew more heavily from what she learned in her home and personal life than what she was taught in the classroom.

The office where she was employed, a staff development training center for special education teachers, had been operating for more than two years under threat of closing due to state and federal budget cutbacks. Overworked and underpaid, the staff labored under the daily tension of not knowing how much longer their jobs would be funded.

At home, Ciampa is the single parent of two teenaged daughters. She puts some 200 miles on her seven-year-old car each week commuting to and from her full-time job, graduate school, and consulting assignments. When she addresses an audience about stress management, she doesn't need to use hypothetical examples. She talks from experience.

"Much of what we call 'stress' comes from feeling we have responsibility and accountability for a situation, but no real control over the outcome. Lots is expected of you, but you don't have the resources to meet those expectations," Ciampa explains. "Often you can't do much about the sources of stress in your life— you can't abruptly quit your job or leave your family—but you can develop new options for *dealing* with stress. One of my solutions was teaching the workshop. Helping other people confront their stress problems put my own into a more manageable perspective.

"I had a strong incentive for developing the workshop," she continues. "It's a subject I needed to know more about in my own life. And in a workshop setting, people confront their problems and generate solutions. The most rewarding aspect of leading a workshop is being a catalyst in this process, and seeing people unleash this potential."

Diane Ciampa knows firsthand the pressures of an impending job layoff, a tight budget, final exams, and single parenthood. But instead of feeling bludgeoned by her problems, she used them as impetus for charting a new phase of her career. And when she addresses an audience, she can say: "I know what you're going through. I have been in your situation. I've tried this, and it works!"

As you evaluate your own credentials for teaching an adult education class or workshop, give yourself plenty of points for "personal experience." Participants want to hear from someone who is actively engaged in the area being taught. If you know *nothing* about the subject in the beginning and learned "from the ground up," as many of your students will, that's even better.

YOU'VE GOT WHAT IT TAKES

What are some of the key personal qualities and character traits of an effective workshop leader? I posed this question to adult education coordinators, professional trainers, and workshop participants. Here is the consensus:

Knowledge in the subject matter. This is a given. Colleen Stafford, who conducts workshops on community organization and leadership skills, believes that "the best trainers, in my opinion, are those who convey the feeling that they know ten times as much about a subject as they had time to tell you. At the end of the program, they leave you wishing for more. (And consequently, you might invite those speakers back for a repeat or an advanced session.)"

In other words, as a workshop leader you create the impression that you have studied your topic extensively so that you could shift through all the divergent viewpoints and nuances and present the main issues and conclusions. It's a tribute to your audience: "I know your time is limited, so I'm just giving you the facts you'll find most relevant."

Knowing your subject thoroughly also adds to your sense of ease and self-confidence. It's the same as when you studied very well for an exam back in high school: You didn't know what the questions would be, but you were relaxed because you were prepared with the answers.

Curiosity. As important as having this base of knowledge in your subject is having a desire to keep learning about it. When a participant asks you a question you can't answer, don't hesitate to respond, "I don't know, but I'll find out." As you constantly improve your presentation with the latest information from new books or newspaper clippings, your presentation takes on a dynamic, up-to-the-minute image. This also communicates:

Enthusiasm. Think back to your high school teachers. Some of them sounded so bored. Their disinterest in their subject was evident in every listless sentence. And there were others who were so enthusiastic that they made *you* care about subjects you frankly never expected to care about. I once sat in on a slide show presentation to a group of dental hygienists. The subject was new methods of preventing gum disease. The participants were captivated, and the evaluations after the session were soaring. One has to conclude it had more to do with the vitality of the presenter, a noted oral surgeon, than the clinical subject matter.

Faye Mapely, a community adult education director who has helped develop and promote hundreds of traditional and offbeat programs for some 20 years, says, "By far the most important quality I look for is enthusiasm. Expertise can be acquired. But enthusiasm has to come from within. It's your enthusiasm that draws people's attention and sustains their interest."

Self-confidence. In the beginning you may have to fake it. It will grow as you gain experience. As people keep referring to you as "the expert," you will gradually start to feel like one. It's like parenthood. The concept is still a bit unreal when the nurse places the newborn infant in your arms. But when the baby looks at you and seems to respond, you feel like a parent. By the time you are being awakened every night for 2 A.M. feedings, your new identity is sealed.

Sense of humor. This doesn't mean a knack for telling jokes but the ability to play spontaneously off someone else's comment, or illustrate your points with appropriate humorous anecdotes. No matter what your subject matter, a little humor seasons it and helps drive the points home. Laughter relaxes your audience, and this puts you at ease as well. It holds people's attention. The heavier the subject, the more a touch of lightness helps.

A sense of humor also keeps you from taking yourself too seriously or becoming overly flustered when a piece of equipment breaks down or a part of your presentation doesn't go over as well as you expected. And that brings up a related issue:

Flexibility. Workshop leaders repeatedly mention the importance of being able to "read the group"; to be able to adapt quickly to the needs and interests of the audience, you need to know when to pursue a line of discussion and when to switch gears.

The value of flexibility was skillfully illustrated in a management seminar I attended. The speaker was lively and knowledgeable, but he had moved to the topic of handling paperwork. Talking about paperwork is about as exciting as dealing with it. The room was stuffy, and we were all feeling the soporific effects of a heavy lunch.

Sensing this—from our slumped shoulders and glazed eyes—our leader said suddenly, "How would you all like to take a crash course in speed reading?" The group sprang back to life. He handed out worksheets with reading exercises and switched on the overhead projector. The turn of events recaptured our attention and made us feel as if we had gotten a bonus—a free set of information beyond what we had expected!

A good workshop leader has many such tricks up the sleeve. An adaptable mind set and a few backup plans help you keep your composure when adversity strikes. The projector jerks to a halt during the opening credits of your 30-minute film. Suddenly you have 25 minutes to fill. Can you do it? You must be able not only to respond to these calamities; you must expect them as well. Then, when things go wrong—and they will—you can congratulate yourself for your foresight.

Showmanship. Would a person who is extremely shy and introverted choose this "limelight" profession? Probably not. But you don't need to be aggressively outgoing either. Many actors and actresses who are quiet and reserved in private life become vivacious and self-possessed in front of an audience. Enthusiasm takes over again, sending out a message of caring and confidence.

In many ways, leading a workshop is like giving a stage performance. You rehearse your best lines and repeat the facts and anecdotes that draw the best audience response. And you use facial expressions, vocal pitch, and body movements just as an actor would, to reinforce your message. Chapter 15 explores these "performance" skills and shows you how to improve your own.

On most occasions you will feel eager to meet your workshop audience and explore your common interests. At other times, you'd give anything to stay home and curl up with a good book. Tough luck. The show must go on. Stage actor and director Robert L. Burpee, who teaches workshops on public-speaking and performing-arts skills, insists:

> You have to muster up the energy and generate that enthusiasm because you owe it to your audience. They don't know or care that you've been sick with bronchitis or that this is the fifth time you've delivered the same talk this week. They are hearing it for the first time. They've paid—with their time if not their money—to be here. Each idea must sound as fresh as the first time it came to you.

Even after you've given the same speech or workshop 20 or 30 times you can prevent it from sounding canned by varying the routine a bit, incorporating new material and soliciting comments from the audience. "At this point I know what I'm going to say and I can anticipate pretty much how people will react, so I vary the *way* I say things," Burpee advises. "I experiment with vocal inflections or pauses in midsentence. That way I can keep myself interested."

Stamina. Standing in front of a group and talking for several hours, even listening and fielding comments, is physically and emotionally exhausting. Your body pumps in enough adrenaline to sustain your energy level through the course of the program, but you can expect to crash when it's over. If you're conducting an all-day workshop, don't plan to do anything too demanding that evening. Eating and sleeping will be sufficient.

A thick skin. Like an actor, as a workshop leader you are going to get some bad reviews, and you can't afford to be overly sensitive. Indeed, you must develop a hide like an alligator. No matter how authoritative and sincere and knowledgeable you are, you won't meet everyone's expectations. People are different. Within any group, the law of averages guarantees that a certain proportion of your audience will be bored or indifferent—even hostile. So expect it. And don't take it too personally.

Chapter Three

What's in It for You?

When you know something good, it's hard to keep it to yourself. There's something intrinsically satisfying about sharing information, whether you're teaching a skill, coaching a team, repeating a rumor, or announcing a promotion.

When you give away money or possessions, it seems to diminish the amount you have. But when you give away knowledge, it grows in volume. The more you impart to others, the more it increases your own store. As the saying goes, teaching is learning. The best way to understand a concept is to have to explain it to others.

Teaching a subject gives you license to really "dig into it," to become an authority on it. You'll add to that store of knowledge with the feedback you get from participants in your class. Their ideas will help you refine your own judgments. Their questions will spur you on to new research.

"Most people teach out of a healthy self-interest, not from a sense of responsibility to help others," observes William A. Draves, national director of LERN, the Learning Resources Network in Manhattan, Kansas. "Teaching, even for free, has many rewards. Brushing up on the subject, 'really understanding' the material, learning from others, and expressing your thoughts are all benefits."

Humans have an inherent need to share knowledge, Draves believes. One reason is that we know more than any previous generation. In the past, ideas were exchanged through the family, church, and other community organizations. Today, participation in these institutions is declining, so we are constantly seeking new avenues of self-expression.[1]

The rewards can be defined as personal and professional, social and psychic. And finally, teaching seminars and workshops can also provide you a very respectable income. I will discuss the financial rewards last in this chapter, because all of the instructors I interviewed insisted that money should be the *last* reason a person should get involved in this business. Your motives, they imply, should be of a higher order.

But, you'll notice, they do not say that money shouldn't be a consideration at all.

VISIBILITY AND CONTACTS

Companies spend billions of dollars sending their key employees through professional development seminars or hiring outside consultants to conduct training programs. Increasingly, large companies are setting up their own in-house training and development departments. As word gets around that you conduct workshops, even on a free-lance or volunteer basis, it can't hurt your professional image. Nor will the conference flyer that lists you as keynote speaker.

Workshops can also boost your business if you are self-employed. Fred S. Steingold and Lonnie L. Loy, an attorney and an accountant, teamed up to present seminars on "How To Start Your Own Small Business." One side benefit is that many of the seminar participants become their clients. Antique dealer Don Johnson gets lots more traffic through his small, out-of-the-way antique shop because he teaches adult education classes on topics like Depression glass and Victorian furniture. His teaching fees are nominal, but the commissions he earns for appraisals more than compensate. People also seek his advice on the value of family heirlooms or bring him items to sell on consignment.

Not everyone who sees your brochure or newspaper ad may sign up for your program, but they may remember your name in the future for some related business. The publicity fixes the idea in people's minds that you are an expert.

Workshops are a congenial way of meeting people and moonlighting your skills without making a full-scale career commitment. You typically contract for one program or series of

---

[1]William A. Draves, *How To Teach Adults* (Manhattan, Kan.: The Learning Resources Network, 1984), p. 2.

classes, often in the evening or on a weekend when it won't interfere with your regular job. It's a business especially well suited to housewives, retired persons, or others who want to work part-time or to make a transition back into the workforce. It can even help lead to a change in careers.

FROM SOCIAL WORKER TO STOCKBROKER

Workshops are often seen as a vehicle for sharing information and helping others. Diane S. Farber carries the thought one step further. It's information to help others make choices.

Like many instructors, she developed her first educational program to answer a need in her own life. "I was going through a divorce," she explains, "and was confronted with decisions about property matters, custody rights—issues I was totally unprepared for and feelings I had not previously experienced."

As a family therapist with a social services agency, Farber knew plenty of other persons who were making similar life transitions. All could benefit, she decided, from an opportunity to share feelings, information, and resources. The workshops on "coping with divorce" served as an educational forum and a support system for both the teacher and participants.

Farber went on to develop other educational programs, notably a series for families dealing with alcoholism. Her premise was the same: The more you know about a subject, the less helpless you feel; the better you can exercise your options.

Soon she was being invited to address professional organizations and civic groups. An authority on alcoholism, she made contacts, gave presentations, gained confidence. When she decided to change careers, she was practicing her own advice: Know your own strengths, get all the facts, and exercise your options.

The move from a family counseling agency to a stock brokerage firm was not the 180-degree switch it first appears. "I still spend much of my time conferring with clients," she points out, "learning about their needs and goals. The difference is, we're talking about financial needs and financial goals."

And she continues to conduct classes and workshops. "Once a workshop junkie, always a workshop junkie," she grins. Her emerging expertise is financial planning for women. Why?

Because women now comprise 50 percent of the workforce and control more than 50 percent of the money in this country. Yet for most women, investment remains a mystique. They tend to keep all of their money in savings accounts or trust funds instead of exploring some means of higher return. I feel women should take more control over their financial resources.

Over time, many of the contacts she makes through giving educational programs are likely to bring her clients. But Farber says she gets an immediate payoff from the people she meets and the feedback she gets. "I really feel that the questions they ask in class are making me a better broker—especially the ones I can't answer! When I don't have the answers, I find them, for all of us."

PSYCHIC REWARDS

It's a heady experience and a little unreal. All week you are an average, inconspicuous person. Then comes the day of the workshop and, like Clark Kent ducking into the phone booth, you don your dress-for-success power suit. Then you gather up your notes and your nerve and arrive at the meeting place. As you walk through the front door, you become ... The Authority. Heads turn. These people have assembled to hear what *you* have to say. They will applaud when you are finished. Even your own mother doesn't applaud after you speak to her.

"It's a very seductive field," warns Tess Kirby, a human resources specialist at a large metropolitan hospital. "Someone asked me what I did for a living recently and I told her I was in the field of training and development. 'Oh yes!' the woman replied. 'The new *glamour* profession!' "

Kirby smiles at the recollection. She had never really thought of her job as glamorous. Like most professional trainers, she spends most of her time behind the scenes: talking with hospital staff members about the educational programs they would like to see offered; drafting proposals; assessing needs; researching her subject; and finally, designing the workshop materials and content. Weeks of preparation go into an average two-hour workshop.

"It's better to be overprepared," Kirby believes. "If you work at your desk and blow a project, maybe you know it and your boss knows. If you're doing a workshop and you don't thoroughly know the material, you blow it in front of 50 people. Besides, I feel a tremendous obligation to the participants. Some workshop instructors will try to bluff their way through. They'll be asked, 'Why is this so?' And they'll reply, 'Because research bears it out.' I think this does a disservice to the participants and the profession."

All those hours of preparation produce deep satisfaction. The payoff: "Exposing people to new and valuable information that they can really use and benefit from. Seeing the 'Aha's' written across their faces! That's a real ego boost," Kirby states.

Those who attend her in-house training programs on communication, motivation, and problem solving recommend it to people in other companies and organizations. As her reputation has grown, so has the steady stream of speaking engagements and consulting work.

And that—for someone who once saw her life within the parameters of "a marriage, 2.5 kids, a dog and a house in the suburbs"—still takes some getting used to.

"It can do strange things to your self-image," she attests. "It's a good thing I have two teenaged sons as a reality check. Let me tell you about a recent experience. . . .

> I was invited to be guest speaker for a local organization's monthly meeting. As I walked into the restaurant, I felt faces turn toward me. "She's *here!*" people said. They rushed toward me to take my coat and offer me a drink. I was introduced to the president of the group and other members. They all acted so grateful to me for coming. All evening I was the center of attention.

> When I arrived home after the meeting was over and stepped out of the car, I thought, that's curious. Where is my red carpet? Why are there not trumpets heralding my arrival? I entered the house, and my sons did not rush up to meet me. Barely looking up from the television, one of them said, "Did you get a chance to wash my jeans, Mom? I need them for school tomorrow." "We're out of milk," greeted the other.

In the end it's like any job, with a mix of highs and lows, glory and drudgery. The unpredictable, multifaceted nature of training and development suits Tess Kirby. "I see life like a wheel. My children, job, friends, spiritual values, professional contacts—all are like spokes of the wheel. If something is wrong with one of the spokes, it throws the whole wheel out of kilter."

Right now the spokes seem to be in good repair; the wheel is moving along at a good pace. "I feel truly blessed," she says, "to be doing something I love and getting paid for it."

THE PROFIT MARGIN

A nationally known management consultant charges $7500 to conduct a week-long seminar on group dynamics. His plane fare, hotel accommodations, meals, and limousine services are extra.

A college professor covers the same topic in a workshop offered as part of a campus "Career Day" conference. She receives a letter of appreciation typed up on a word processor.

You're an expert on group dynamics yourself. What kind of fee can you expect?

The answer, as you've probably guessed, is: that depends.

The value of your program is contingent on so many things: your reputation and your credentials; the competition, and what they are charging; the popularity of your subject; what the market, in your particular community, will bear.

People will pay more for your program if they believe it will bring them a long-term payoff. For example, many creative-writing seminars offer instruction on literary style and content. Jeanne Paul teaches a writing course with a different angle: "Freelance Writing for Glory and Profit" emphasizes marketing.

Some students even commute 60 or 70 miles for her course because she has something they want: information on how to *sell* what they write. One or two sales could make up the cost of tuition, they figure. Besides, the course fee is a tax-deductible business expense.

Jeanne Paul has proven herself in the area she is teaching. She has been published in a string of prominent newspapers and magazines. She was a ghostwriter for a U.S. Senator and is a former syndicated columnist. So students know that she isn't hypothesizing about the writing business, but speaking from experience.

Larry Kokkelenberg has amassed credentials of a different sort. As president of his own Chicago-based consulting firm, he conducts seminars on topics like needs analysis, team building, and personnel-hiring assessment. At one firm, he is credited with reducing employee turnover by 400 percent! His fees are in the $600–$1100 per day bracket. Can you see some company paying $1000 per day for your services? It will, if its officers are convinced that your program will increase their productivity and profits.

Fame helps. Danny Simon's workshop, "The Craft of Comedy Writing for Television," always fills up because, hey, this is a chance to hear tips from a real pro—someone who has written for the likes of Sid Caesar, Phil Silvers, and Milton Berle. There is an aura about someone who keeps such company and who is the brother of the playwright Neil Simon. People enroll with the anticipation of breaking into the big time, the lucrative world of television screenwriting. But they also enjoy the show business stories and the personal anecdotes he tells. Three days with Danny Simon isn't just instruction; it's entertainment.

But you don't have to be known or notable if you are offering a unique, intriguing course on a topic that no one else has thought of. That's what Charlie Jones did. Back in the mid-1970s, Jones came up with a workshop on Job Burnout, a phrase that apparently struck a chord of recognition with a large part of the population. Suddenly, everyone was talking about it. "What is it?" "Have I got it?" And people flocked to Jones's seminars to find out what to do about it. The moral: If you can be the first on your block to offer a course on a popular hot topic, you may be able to quickly move into a higher income bracket.

In sum, you can charge more for your program if it enables participants to:

Make more money.

Become more productive.

Feel more in control of their lives.

Or you can charge more if you, the presenter, are:

Proven in your field.

Famous.

Published.

First, with a subject that's fascinating.

All of which brings us back to the basic question: "How much?" How much can you charge for your seminar when you're just breaking into the business? I have given this question a lot of thought, and my answer is: Ask someone else.

Seek the opinions of consultants in your community who are roughly equivalent to you in experience and expertise. Try to find out what your direct competitors charge. What's the going rate that local companies pay outside consultants? An organization that might help you make these connections is the American Society for Training and Development. If there isn't a chapter in your area, start one.

There's a fine line between charging too little, and creating the impression that you're an amateur, and charging too much, pricing yourself right out of the market.

Sandra Johnson, a 42-year-old nurse/nutritionist, made inquiries of this sort while planning her course in preventive health care. She determined that for her, the "right" fee registered at $50 per hour.

> I had taught courses in health and nutrition in California, but I was affiliated with a university there. Now I had moved with my family to New York, and decided to try it on my own. I had to come up with a pay scale that was compatible with what others were charging and with what I felt my services were worth. Twenty-five dollars seemed too low. At that, I'd barely break even after allowing for preparation time, materials, and other equipment. But I couldn't hear myself charging $100 per hour either! An inner voice kept saying, "$100? You? Be serious!"

A year later, however, Johnson was getting $100 per hour and more for her highly entertaining and motivating program on personal health and well-being. Once she had established a reputation she was signed on by a prominent speakers bureau, which had no trouble eliciting higher fees.

Ultimately, you weigh the comparative values of money versus time. Curtis Van Voorhees, a University of Michigan professor of education and private consultant, was in his late twenties when he developed a program he calls "Personal Achievement"—his own blending of self-awareness, goal setting, and motivation. Almost immediately, the seminar took off, and through word-of-mouth publicity Van Voorhees was getting a steady stream of speaking requests.

> At one point, I found myself booked solid for two weeks, giving the same presentation from Alaska to Colorado to Connecticut. It was a great experience and it was exhausting. I thought, "I can't keep this up. It's taking too much time away from my job and my family." So I decided: "I'll double my fees and I'll probably get half as many requests. That way I'll maintain the same level of income, but spend half as much time on the road.
>
> You know what happened? As soon as I raised my fees, the requests for my program doubled!"

Three other highly successful national consultants related identical experiences. As the saying goes, "you get what you pay for."

And some people feel, accurately or not, that a lower price tag means an inferior product. The reverse psychology also applies. If something costs a bit more, it must be special. It is probably worth it.

Find a fee that seems to be the right "fit" for you. Try it on for a year. If you're good, you'll get referrals and repeat business. As your reputation and self-confidence moves up a notch, give yourself a raise. You've earned it.

GETTING WHAT YOU'RE WORTH

One thing is for sure. Your clients—whether they are individuals signing up for your workshop or companies hiring you as a consultant—expect value; a fair return on their investment. They're not looking for a bargain. So set a fair price for your time and effort, and give them their money's worth.

Remember that when you serve as a private consultant, your fees for the hours you are working must sustain you for the hours you're not. They must compensate for preparation time, developing slides and transparencies, assembling handouts. They must also cover advertising costs, telephone charges, office equipment. So before you think, "I can't charge $500 a day," total up your expenses. You may find you can't afford *not* to charge $500. Don't feel sheepish about it.

Women seem to have an especially hard time asking a fair payment for their services. We are so used to chairing committees and counseling others on a volunteer basis that many of us feel vaguely uneasy about getting paid for it. Sometimes you'll want to donate your services to a nonprofit organization or church group. But when a local corporation asks you to conduct an inservice training session, that's a different matter. Your invoice will hardly make an impact on their annual profit-and-loss statement.

Francine Surgerer, owner of Communitec, Inc., a company that specializes in technical-writing services and seminars, recalls, "I practiced in front of the mirror, stating over and over again, 'I charge $$X00$ per day plus expenses. I charge $$X00$ per day . . . ' until I could say it without faltering."

If it makes you feel any better, those people who call to request your services feel just as awkward as you do about the subject of money. Maybe they are afraid if they offer you too much, you'll take advantage of them; if they propose too low a stipend, you may feel insulted.

A good way for you to bridge this communications gap is to inquire, at some point in the discussion:

"How much do you have budgeted for this event?"

This gives both of you room to negotiate. If they say, "we can spend $200," tell them what kind of program you can provide for $200.

Another approach is to offer a choice: your standard seminar and your deluxe model. "I include selected handout materials as part of this fee. But if you prefer, I can provide a 40-page resource notebook at an additional $5 per participant."

SHOULD YOU GIVE IT AWAY?

If only potential contractors and clients were lined up with fists full of dollars, outbidding one another for your services. "We want you!" the throngs insist. "State your terms! Name your price!" Alas, in the real world, you can expect many calls like these:

> "Unfortunately, our club doesn't have any money in its treasury for an honorarium, but we'd like you to be our guest for dinner."

> "Since we're a nonprofit group, we are hoping you'd conduct the workshop as a, you know, community service."

> "Here at the Adult Learning Network, we charge between $10 and $15 for most of our courses. We split 50–50 with the teacher. So if ten people sign up for your course, you could make as much as $50!"

Should you do freebies? Should you charge lower rates for some groups than for others? Absolutely. Especially when you're just starting out in the business.

Johnson, Van Voorhees, Surgerer, and all of the consultants I surveyed were unanimous on this point. "Look at it as good exposure and practical experience," says Surgerer, a frequent guest speaker at professional meetings and conferences. "My motivation is to develop interest in Communitec, give myself some visibility, and try out some teaching techniques.

"You can spend $500 in a newspaper display ad promoting your talents. Or you could speak for free at a national conference and get $500 worth of national exposure in the conference program and newspaper writeups."

Van Voorhees adds, "Practically every talk you give may lead to new business. It's worth it to drive 50 miles to address 50 members of the Rotary Club if it ultimately brings in several thousand dollars of consulting contracts."

A footnote to that advice: Whenever you do a speaking engagement, bring business cards. Better yet, provide handouts that prominently display your name, phone number, and range of services.

As you become more established, you will want to devise a uniform fee schedule. You don't want the members of two different organizations comparing notes. "She charged us $250 for a half-day seminar." "She did? No kidding! We got her for $75!"

The key is to be consistent, yet flexible. You can continue to accept free or nominal-fee engagements when it's for a cause you believe in or when it's in your best interests. But make it known that you are making an exception. "My usual fee is $250, but I make it a policy to contribute my services gratis for a few non-profit organizations such as yours."

Donating your services can be very rewarding. It's free publicity, good practice, and excellent public relations.

Chapter Four

What's in It for Them?

Ask a child why he's going to school, and he'll likely respond: "Because I have to." Adults will give you a much more positive reason. They come back to school because they *want* to.

There are exceptions, of course. Some people may be sent to your program by their boss or brought in tow by an insistent spouse. Some may come more out of curiosity than impassioned interest. And many will be skeptical that you can deliver all that you promise. Still, the vast majority of participants are as optimistic as you are that this will be a rewarding experience.

This puts you at a distinct advantage. You don't have to win them over. But you do have to sustain their interest.

Before you refine your topic or design the workshop, look at the project from the participant's point of view. Why would they want to attend? What do they hope to get out of it?

Their motivation probably stems from a number of sources—the same ones, in fact, that gave rise to the boom in adult education in general. Here's a brief recap:

WHY PEOPLE ENROLL IN CLASSES AND WORKSHOPS

To broaden their base of knowledge and experience

To meet people who share similar values and interests

To learn how to make or save more money

To keep up with technological advances in their fields

To acquire skills that will qualify them for better jobs or to change careers

To have fun

To improve their personal quality of life

Will the program you are planning respond to these needs? At least four out of seven? Then you're off and running!

THE DIFFERENCE WITH GROWNUPS

Before you rush up to the podium and face these eager throngs, perhaps you should know something about them. Many of us have had some experience in teaching children—as leaders of youth groups and even as parents. Some of the same instructional principles that work with children can be transferred to adults. For example, people of all ages respond to praise, recognition, and rewards.

But adults are different than children. Besides being taller and sometimes smarter, they have certain physical and intellectual characteristics that influence the learning process. I will focus on five traits that have particular implications for you, the prospective teacher. They are: experience, habits, dignity, anatomy, and time consciousness.

Experience.   The people who come to your workshop may think they have no preconceived notions of what will take place. But in fact, they have a whole battery of hopes, biases, and expectations. They have their own ideas about what they would like to learn, and most important, they have a lifetime of wisdom to contribute.

"A child's mind is like a clean slate," explains one fourth-grade teacher turned adult educator. "In elementary school, much of what you teach children are brand new concepts which they have never before confronted. But an adult must integrate whatever new ideas you are presenting with everything they've learned in the past."

As a teacher, this can work for you or against you. In a workshop on "Living with Your Teenager," the astute teacher helps parents reach back into their own past to remember how they felt as adolescents, coping with high school, peer pressure, and other growing pains. Experience can be a very good teacher.

But it can also make us set in our ways. "Computer phobia is a very real thing," observes a young man who teaches programming classes to groups of preschool children and their parents. "Some adults look at a computer terminal and physically freeze. To many people, new technology represents a 'dehuman-ized' office place, lost jobs and other changes and problems." He finds that the young children take to computers as ducks to water. Many adults still find them rather threatening.

In some workshops you may face the extra challenge of dis-mantling old ideas in order to make way for new ones. You may have to persuade participants to give up or at least modify "the way we've always, always done it."

An effective workshop allows for plenty of free-flowing dis-cussion in which people can express their reservations and ask questions. There are three payoffs: (1) It gives them time to process the information you're sharing and link it with their own past experiences. (2) Drawing on that experience, many mem-bers of the group will be able to solve one another's problems. (3) At least, it lets each participant discover, "Aha! So I'm not the only person who feels this way!"

Habits. In the course of accruing years of experience, adults form habits and nice, comfortable routines. For example, we get up in the morning, get dressed, go to work and, at some point, most of us start the day with a cup of coffee. If you're conducting a morning workshop, be sure to supply that coffee. Provide hot water for those who prefer decaffeinated coffee or tea. And pro-vide a midmorning break so that people can refill their cups.

Smoking is another habit you must contend with, and a po-tentially more contentious one. Coffee drinkers and nondrinkers coexist very compatibly. Smokers and nonsmokers may forge themselves into armed camps. The cookbook solution is: If it's a large group (50 or more), you can try to accommodate both fac-tions by dividing the room into smoking and nonsmoking sec-tions. In smaller groups, let the participants themselves decide. Compromises are usually possible.

Be sensitive to behavioral habits also. Some people custom-arily take a seat in the very front of the room. Others prefer to hide in the back rows where they feel inconspicuous and com-fortable. You won't endear yourself by insisting that they march down to the front seats.

Most people choose to sit in the rear as a matter of habit, not disinterest. Don't be concerned about it. Respect people's idio-syncrasies and accommodate them.

Dignity. Adults have dignity. In other words, treat them as adults. Adults don't want to be told where to sit or what to do or how to behave. They came for advice and information, not rules.

Some adult educators err by coming across as dictatorial or patronizing. ("I am the font of knowledge, and all of you are mere empty vessels waiting to receive my pearls of wisdom.") You can be authoritative without being authoritarian. An effective workshop leader values the experience of the audience and welcomes their contributions. Never even hint that your students are inferior or inadequate. Downplay the possibility that they are even mistaken.

Some people return to the classroom because of perceived shortcomings in themselves, but once they are there, they don't wish to be reminded of them. Focus on the positive. Learning takes place in an atmosphere of mutual respect, where all ideas and opinions are welcomed.

Anatomy.   Children have short, flexible bodies that can be propped up at a desk for three hours at a stretch. They can even sit on the floor. Most adult bodies become very uncomfortable after sitting even half that long, unless they are asleep. And if they're asleep, you've got another kind of problem.

Adults are also more sensitive to other kinds of discomfort. Cigarette smoke is one. A room that is chilly, stuffy, poorly lit, or too noisy is also distracting. Pay attention to visibility and acoustics. And never go longer than 90 minutes without taking a break.

In comfortable physical surroundings, participants can concentrate on the workshop content, not the environment.

Time consciousness.   Some people may enroll in your class because the hours weigh heavily and they have nothing better to do. This may be true of 3, even 5 percent. The other 95 percent are busy, if not swamped, with other commitments. They are investing one of their most precious commodities, their time, by attending, and they are expecting results.

Workshops and other types of short-term training evolved, in fact, in response to people's need for practical information condensed into a relatively short time frame. If we had all the time in the world, we might audit a college psychology course in order to better understand human nature. Instead, we opt for a three-hour seminar on "Improving Relationships."

Most workshops tend to be problem oriented, and so do the participants. When people sign up for "Dealing with Drug Dependency" or "Tax-Deferred Investments," they are looking for answers to real-life situations. In most cases, they are motivated

about their jobs, families, or other personal issues
le workshop to suggest some new options.

3,179,0

is no less important to persons who enroll in what
ned "personal enrichment courses." Music appreci-

4.99 T 1

apsychology are not problem centered; they appeal

5.99 T 1

of learning for learning's sake. Students in these

66 Tx

le hoping to acquire new knowledge or an enlight-

11.64 CT

—but they too expect their time to be well spent.

20.04 TO

ave just stayed home and curled up with an ency-

8.40 CG

:ive workshop leader pays homage to the partici-

D   54.40

essures by:

and ending on time.

- Pacing the content so that the group doesn't spend too much time
  on any one activity or topic. It's better to hit the high points of an
  issue and whet people's curiosity than to belabor it until they lose
  interest.
- Providing specific steps and plans that can be applied to real-life
  situations.

Good workshops don't just raise issues. They solve problems.

HOW ADULTS LEARN

I hear, and I forget.
I see, and I remember.
I do, and I understand.

(Old Chinese Proverb)

Volumes of research studies, whole library shelves, are devoted
to the subject of how adults learn. Many of the theoretical and
physiological issues—such as right-brain creativity versus left-
brain logic—are still being debated, but the experts seem to agree
on several points:

1. Adults must *want* to learn in the first place. We need to see long-
   range or (preferably) immediate personal benefits.
2. Adults learn by doing. For information to "stick," we need an opportunity to put it into practice.
3. Adults learn differently from one another, and most of us respond
   to a variety of teaching methods.

Dean N. Osterman, director of instructional and faculty development at Oregon State University, suggests that adult learners may be grouped in four categories. The four groups emerge from his research and teaching of adults, using such instruments as the Learning Style Inventory, created by Bernice McCarthy of EXCEL, Inc., and the writings of Carl Jung. Here is a breakdown of these four adult learning groups:

Type One: The Feelers.   They seek meaningful applications of the knowledge that is presented. They learn by listening and sharing ideas. When there is diversity of opinion within a group, they look for a consensus. They learn best through one-on-one discussion and personal involvement. Their favorite question is *Why?* The teaching method they respond best to is the discussion group.

Type Two: The Thinkers.   Analytical and pragmatic, they seek straightforward facts and information. They are data collectors. They might tend to become impatient during a prolonged group discussion, because they do not come to a workshop to hear opinions of other participants; they want to hear from the expert. They are less interested in people than in ideas and concepts. Their favorite question is *What?* The best teaching method for them is the lecture format.

Type Three: The Sensors.   They are guided by common sense in their efforts to understand how things work. Skip the theory for them; they are interested in practical applications. They learn by testing ideas, and they would much rather solve a problem than be given the answer. They enjoy short five-minute problem-solving exercises with clearly defined procedures and objectives. *How?* is their favorite question. An effective teaching device for them is the one-on-one coaching method or a good demonstration followed by immediate application.

Type Four: The Intuitors.   Innovative, self-motivated, they look for alternatives to traditional learning situations. They are risk takers, attracted by situations that involve variety and flexibility. They learn well by trial and error and self-discovery. The intuitors like to make things happen. They bring action to concepts and carry out goals. Their favorite question is *If . . . ?* They learn through pre- and postactivity tests and guided challenges.

To illustrate further the difference in learning styles, Osterman uses a brick as a model. "What would you do with a brick?" he asks.

Type Ones would discuss all its possible uses, arrive at a consensus, and use it in harmonious colors to build a useful structure. Or, they might wrap it in bright paper and use it as a paperweight.

Type Twos would analyze it to see how much it weighs, what colors it comes in, and measure its length, depth, width, and other dimensions.

Type Threes would build a barbecue, or use it as a door stop.

And Type Fours would look for imaginative new uses for the brick. They might use it to wash an elephant.

What type of learner are you? What types are most of your students? In a one-day workshop, or even a short series of classes, you probably won't get an opportunity to discover each person's best learning style. So the most effective, dynamic learning program offers something for everyone.

"Accommodate the squares and the pegs," Osterman advises, "—large and small group discussions for the Ones; 20-minute lectures for the Twos; short problem-solving exercises, with coaching, for the Threes; tests, guided challenges, and take-home experiments for the Fours."

Chapter Five offers some guidelines for incorporating many teaching approaches into your own workshop. In Chapter Seven, we sit in on one of Dean Osterman's own workshops, where you can see how he puts his own theories into practice.

Chapter Five

Researching and Designing Your Program

You've chosen a topic, gathered the information, and targeted the audience. Now, how do you put these ideas across in a clear, logical sequence?

You can't just go in and start talking. Every speech, class, or workshop requires planning and preparation. At the very beginning of your preparations, consider the following:

What are the goals of this program? Are you aiming to:

Train participants in new skills?

Motivate them to work harder?

Change their attitudes?

Impart new information?

Solve some problems?

Build a sense of camaraderie or group solidarity?

Write out your objectives, just as they might appear on a brochure to be circulated among potential participants. Put yourself in their place. What would motivate them to attend? Plan your program, not based around how much you know, but around what you hope your audience will gain from attending.

Who Is Your Audience?

Are they mostly male, female, or a mixed group?

What are their general ages and education levels?

Do they have any background at all in your subject?

Do they work together, or are they otherwise acquainted?

Will they be meeting for the first time, as strangers?

How large is the group that is expected?

How much time and money is it costing them?

Remember that your audience brings a wide variety of skills and experience to your program. They are not just a sounding board for your knowledge, but a resource, with their own agenda and ideas. Two seminars on investment strategies may contain the same information, but the focus will differ dramatically between a group of rising business executives and an audience of retired couples.

Three other factors that affect your program design include facilities, timing, and equipment. Chapter Eight addresses these items in detail, but it's not too soon to begin thinking about the following:

Where will the workshop take place? The location where you'll be speaking makes a difference in setting the tone for your presentation. The same words come across differently in a formal restaurant or meeting hall than in a church basement.

Seating arrangements either encourage or inhibit participant involvement. Will your audience be stiffly seated in columns of straight-backed chairs? Or will they be lounging in a semicircle, cross-legged on the floor?

When will it be held? Participants come with different expectations to a morning workshop that absorbs part of their workday than they do for an after-dinner presentation or an evening seminar. An equally relevant time factor is: How long will it last?

What about equipment? Will you be using props, handouts, visual aids? Begin thinking now about how they will fit in with the workshop format. Don't just plug them in at the end.

All of these seemingly peripheral issues have an effect on the workshop style and content.

If you are conducting your program for some sponsoring agency, whether a company, a conference, or a community organization, many of these details will be handled for you. If you are mounting the program on your own, you must see to them yourself, along with such matters as publicity and promotion. But even if someone else is making the arrangements, it's your responsibility to verify them. Learn all you can in advance about your audience, your facilities, and your resources. On the day of your program, you want to leave as little to chance as possible.

RESEARCHING AND ORGANIZING YOUR TOPIC

Now that you've considered the who, when, where, and why of your program, we return to the central questions of *what* and *how*.

There is no easy formula that can be applied to designing a workshop, because each one is so different. A program on assertiveness training will obviously be conducted differently than one on furniture refinishing or weightlifting. Nevertheless, most workshops and short courses have these characteristics in common:

- The information is presented in a logical sequence.
- The instructor employs a variety of teaching methods.
- The participants have an opportunity to practice what they have learned.
- Practical application is emphasized over theoretical concepts.

Even a workshop on "How to Flirt" plays up the practical aspects of the program content.

Stage One: Gathering Information

Since you've been asked to make a presentation or conduct a workshop, you are already, one presumes, fairly knowledgeable on the workshop topic. At the very minimum, you are sufficiently intrigued by it and willing to do as much research as necessary in order to sound informed and authoritative when you stand before an audience.

Ultimately, you'll pull information from many sources: books, magazine articles, statistical surveys, research reports, your own personal experience, and the experience of other people. Allow yourself several weeks for this process.

Start by preparing a rough outline of the basic points you wish to cover. This is your topic agenda. Carry it with you along with a notebook or a pack of index cards so that whenever you think of an idea you want to include in the workshop, you can jot it down. Don't worry about organization at this stage.

Next, head for the library and check out whatever books you can find on the topic. The *Guide to Periodic Literature* will steer you to recent magazine articles, which are likely to contain some of the most current information. A speechwriter's sourcebook of anecdotes or popular quotations might provide some nuggets of wisdom to work into your opening or closing comments. Talk to the reference librarians. They can guide you to almanacs, statistical surveys, and other facts and data sources.

Your third valuable information resource is people. Interview specialists in the subject area. Ask your friends and business associates what they would like to learn if they were attending your workshop. Who else do they suggest you talk to? Devise and circulate a questionnaire. Gather a group of creative people for a brainstorming session. Make it worth their time. Buy lunch.

Later, as you are conducting the workshop, you'll collect relevant data from another important resource: your audience. Their questions and comments will be grist for future workshops. The more people you survey, the more you'll notice a consensus about the issues that most people find most relevant. You can truthfully say to your audience: "The question that is most often raised is . . . " or, "The main problems in this field seem to be . . ." Each time you give your presentation, it will be more tightly focused on the participants' concerns.

Stage Two: Honing It Down

Researching is the fun part. You could probably continue it indefinitely, at least as long as your curiosity holds out. But as the date of the presentation approaches, you must suspend the information gathering and begin molding it into a coherent training program.

Be selective. It isn't possible to tell the audience everything that has ever been said about the topic. Think of each fact, anecdote, or concept as a building block in your presentation. Assess each block for shape and substance. Will it strengthen or enliven the final product? Or does it just add dead weight? Before you include any piece of information, ask:

Is it interesting?
Is it accurate?
Is it relevant?

To each of these questions, attach the phrase, ". . . to the audience." This is where "knowing your audience" becomes imperative. What you decide to include depends on how much they know about the topic already. Target their concerns. Emphasize the information that will benefit them.

As you assemble these bits and blocks of information, you'll see that they sort themselves into categories. For example:

> Historical or chronological events (lay the foundation for the material to be presented)
>
> Surprising statistics (grab attention, arouse interest)
>
> Anecdotes, case studies (illustrate key points, relate to audience)
>
> Issues and problems (acknowledge or create audience needs)
>
> Solutions (provide several alternatives to satisfying the needs)

You can use any method you wish for organizing your material, but the index card approach—used in the writing of college term papers—works as well as any. Each piece of information you wish to include is printed on a 3- by 5-inch card. The cards are grouped under various headings. The headings are arranged in a logical sequence.

At the end, your data blocks "build" from a solid foundation of information, arouse interest, create a need, pinpoint problems, and propose solutions. You've created a flexible workshop agenda that can be adjusted to fit any audience.

VARY YOUR TEACHING STYLES

Whatever its length, every presentation has three parts:

1. The introduction. You capture attention, outline goals for the session, establish a good learning climate, and motivate your audience to fully participate.
2. The body. Everything in between.
3. The conclusion. You may recap your major points; summarize what has been learned or accomplished; evaluate the learning experience.

The introduction and the conclusion of your workshop may take five or ten minutes apiece. But the middle could fill several hours—or several days. During this time, plan to use a variety of teaching methods.

As discussed in Chapter Four, people are not alike. We behave differently and we learn differently. By using a variety of teaching approaches within your workshop, you strengthen the odds that at least one of those approaches will be effective for most of your audience. You also create a much more interesting, dynamic learning environment. Here are some of your options.

Lecture

This is the most common and traditional teaching method. It's simple too. You present the facts and concepts; the group sits passively and listens. Even note-taking is optional. All that is really required is staying awake.

The advantage of the lecture is that it allows you to deliver a maximum amount of information within a relatively short time frame. But while this appears very efficient, it may not be the most effective. Adults learn better when they are actively involved. They need an opportunity to process the information and see how it applies to them personally. If you want your audience to really retain an idea, give them a chance to discuss it and put it into practice.

Still, your workshop has to include some lecturing. At the beginning of the program, for example, you must introduce the topic. You can't just start off saying, "Hi! What would you like to talk about?" So when the program calls for a lecture format, you can increase student involvement by doing the following:

Use visual aids. Props, flipcharts, and other devices help to clarify and illustrate your talk. Even a few key words on the blackboard serve to direct the group's thinking and reinforce your message.

Keep it simple. Avoid the use of jargon or phrases that sound stuffy and academic. An informal, conversational style and short, clear sentences will communicate your ideas most effectively.

Get feedback. Don't just talk at the audience. Challenge them. Provoke them. Ask questions: "How many of you think ... ?" "Would you agree that ... ?" Nodding heads and a show of hands assures you that they are paying attention.

Discussion

One of the surest ways to increase participant involvement is to follow your lecture with a discussion period. It gives your audience an opportunity to expand on one or more of your ideas, to request clarification, express disagreement, and to exchange ideas with one another.

Discussions come in many sizes and shapes.

Diad. Participants discuss an issue in pairs; usually, two persons seated next to one another. Easy and nonthreatening, three-minute diads make a good icebreaking activity.

Triad.   A diad plus one.

Buzz groups.   Four or five persons are generally considered an optimal number for generating ideas or conclusions on a given subject. Buzz groups can be formed quickly. ("Okay, move your chairs and get together in groups of five.") You may wish to give each group a sheet of newsprint on which they can write, in large legible words, their consensus. You then tape the newsprint sheets on the wall as a focal point for the full-group discussion.

Full-group discussion.   The group reassembles, and you're back at the helm, fielding questions, opinions, and responses. It takes some skill to elicit comments from the shy participants, to control the monopolizers, and to keep the discussion from trailing off on a tangent. Full-group discussions are most manageable in groups of 25 or fewer. The smaller the group, the less reticent people are about speaking up.

Brainstorming.   In this method, you raise an issue and ask participants to suggest, quickly and spontaneously, any and all problems and/or solutions. You record them on the blackboard or newsprint chart. Anything goes. All suggestions are duly noted without comment or criticism. Afterward, the whole group evaluates them.

Bull session.   Informal, spontaneous, and generally leaderless, this form of discussion may be useful for group consciousness-raising or problem solving. It may be too freewheeling for many workshop formats. If you are working within a limited time frame, it's probably more productive to stick with more structured forms of discussion and encourage the group to hold bull sessions on their own time—perhaps over lunch.

Demonstration

Some types of workshops emphasize doing, not discussing. This category ranges from on-the-job training for new plant employees to ballroom dancing or first aid. Most courses in arts and crafts, home, or practical skills call for the demonstration method. You would not give a lecture on how to make a macrame plant hanger—you'd show how it's done.

This requires two kinds of talent: first, proficiency in your particular area of interest, and second, the ability to break it down into clear, logical steps and to explain the steps patiently to others.

To be truly effective, a demonstration should be followed by the opportunity for practice and feedback. Coaching is the most individualized approach, allowing you to give personalized attention to each of the participants as they carry out your instructions. Demonstration workshops usually have limited enrollments so that teachers can provide this kind of one-on-one assistance.

Role Play

Role play can be a powerful teaching and learning device. As the demonstration method lets you practice a new craft or skill, role play enables you to practice a new behavior. With an instructor's guidance, participants usually work in small groups and act out situations that simulate a real-life experience. The scripts may be written out, but they are usually ad-libbed or improvised.

The method was put to good use in an assertiveness-training workshop I attended. Following a general discussion of social interaction and behavior styles, we were divided into small groups of six participants plus one facilitator. We each described situations in which we felt intimidated. Our problems ranged from dealings with rude salesclerks to asking for a raise.

One member of our group was Brenda, a shy, quiet young woman in her late twenties who had recently been made supervisor of her department at a large hospital. One of the orderlies was a surly man twice her size and old enough, he informed her, to be her father. He was openly resentful of taking orders from a young woman.

"What kind of things does he say to you? How do you respond?" the facilitator asked. With the help of the group, Brenda devised a new strategy for communicating with the dissident staff member, looking him straight in the eye and speaking to him with coolness and authority. One of the men in our group played the role of the orderly, and Brenda practiced her new approach with him until she could say her lines without faltering. The advice and encouragement she got from the group gave her visible self-confidence.

In many workshops, role play activities are enhanced by videotape players. The "instant replays" allow us to see ourselves as others see us. They are particularly effective in workshops on public speaking, job interviewing, and other communication skills.

A cautionary note: Role play, role reversals, videotaped playbacks, and other kinds of skits and simulations require a special degree of sensitivity and skill on the part of the trainer.

You must create an atmosphere of trust, in which participants can let down their inhibitions. Even so, some will balk at the idea of "performing." If some prefer to observe, leave them that option.

Exercises, Games, and Other Activities

A short quiz, a fill-in-the-blank worksheet, a simulation game or case study—all provide a change of pace from the traditional lecture/discussion format. These activities can serve as a valuable adjunct because they enable participants to practice and apply the information you have presented.

Written exercises are easy to devise and administer. For example, in a career-planning workshop, you might include a test aimed at measuring personal values, or have participants list their long-range professional goals. In a money management course, have participants fill out their own balance sheet of income and expenses. Unlike role play and discussion sessions, which require active involvement, written exercises are inner-directed and totally nonthreatening. People like them because they enjoy tuning in to their own thoughts and experiences.

Case studies or "trigger films" depicting a real-life situation related to the workshop theme can be used to direct thinking or spark a discussion. "In-basket" exercises, in which participants tackle a stack of paperwork or a series of problems in sequence, are a lesson in creative decision making and priority setting. And finally, simulation games, used extensively by the military for devising defense strategies and field maneuvers, have moved into the general education area. Business simulations are incorporated in many management-training seminars. They give rising executives an opportunity to test their initiative and problem-solving skills in situations that closely match those they may encounter on the job. Games may be more costly in terms of time, special equipment, or auxiliary personnel. But as learning experiences they can be profoundly effective.

WRITE YOUR OWN SCRIPT

In developing my time management workshop, I found it helpful to sit down at the typewriter and outline an entire script for the material I wished to present. I don't mean that I wrote out every spoken sentence ("Hello, my name is . . ."). I just used phrases and key words that would cue me to the main points I wished to cover.

Getting the material out of my head and on paper, in a concrete, visible form, I could then arrange the subject matter in a logical sequence. I could better estimate how much time to plan for each topic and see which topics lent themselves to various teaching methods. Here's how it looked:

Sample Script for a Morning Time Management Workshop

TIME	METHOD	TOPICS
8:15–9:00		(Preparations, set up)
9:00–9:10	lecture	Give short introduction of myself, my approach to time management, goals of the course.
9:10–9:20	warmup	Participants briefly tell their names, where they work, what they hope to learn.
9:20–9:30	brainstorming exercise	Ask group how they tend to waste time now. What they want more time for. Stress universal nature of time problems, common goals of participants.
9:30–9:45	written exercise	Give time management quiz to show participants their current strong points and weaknesses. Discuss answers and scores.
9:45–10:00	buzz groups	Divide into groups of five to identify major time wasters. Reassemble and report to whole group. This creates a specific agenda for issues we will discuss. (Some groups have the biggest problems with

TIME	METHOD	TOPICS
		meetings and paperwork. Others would rather talk about housework.)
10:00–10:20	lecture and feedback	Using flip chart, I describe strategies for setting goals and priorities. Showing props such as appointment calendars and "To Do" lists, I discuss ways these tools can help people schedule activities and get more done. Group offers ideas based on personal experience.
10:20–10:30	written exercise	On blank piece of paper, each person writes out a "To Do" list for tomorrow, ranks tasks by priority, and plans a "perfect day" for him/herself.
10:30–10:40		(Break)
10:40–11:00	lecture and feedback	Explain concept of physiological energy rhythms and idea of preserving your "prime time" of day for most demanding, high-priority activities; your "down time" for routine busy work.
	written exercise	If time, have them chart their own energy cycles on graph paper.
11:00–11:30	lecture, with anecdotes, case studies	Present methods of dealing with each of the time wasters listed earlier, includ-

TIME	METHOD	TOPICS
		ing telephone calls, drop-in visitors, meetings, etc. Get more tips from participants.
11:30–11:35	two-person buzz groups	In pairs, have participants discuss psychological time wasters: indecision, worry, guilt, perfectionism, and procrastination.
11:35–11:55	lecture and discussion	Ask group for examples of above problems. Discuss strategies for dealing with them.
11:55–noon	lecture and feedback	Give summary and closing thoughts. Ask participants to complete evaluations. Distribute remaining handouts. Thank everyone for coming.

An outline such as this can help you conceptualize the points you wish to emphasize, the order in which to present them, and how much time to allot to each. Think of it as a flexible framework, not a mold cast in iron. Each individual activity is like an accordion. It can be stretched or compressed as time allows or as the interests of the group dictate.

By incorporating more learning-by-doing activities, longer group discussions, and a short film, I can expand this morning's program to a full-day workshop or a five-week adult education course. I can also use the individual topics as the grist of a 30-minute speech.

This kind of preparation is time-consuming. But once you've developed the basic blueprint, you can reuse it, revise it, and continue to improve on it.

Chapter Six

Facilitating Discussions

A discussion group is like an airplane. It's one thing to be able to define it, as we did in the last chapter. It's quite another to be able to get it off the ground. And it takes real skill to keep it from going off course.

Still, a free-flowing, stimulating discussion is central to an effective adult learning experience. In fact, without this exchange of ideas, your program would be a speech, not a workshop. Discussion shifts some responsibility from the leader to the learners. You can relax for a minute and let someone have the floor. It's a bit unpredictable—you never know what someone in the group is going to say. But for that very reason, it holds attention and gets everyone involved.

What makes for a good discussion?

- The atmosphere is relaxed and nonthreatening. No one is afraid to offer an opinion for fear of sounding foolish. (This is sometimes difficult to achieve in a workshop attended by several levels of employees within one company. People are often reluctant to speak candidly when their supervisor is present.)

- There is a sense of common purpose. The issue is relevant to everyone in the group, not just to one or two persons and not just to the discussion leader. How can you tell if it holds their interest? Check the body language. Slumped shoulders and bored or wandering glances spell apathy. When you see these signs, don't pretend to ignore them. Switch gears. Say, "I sense you're ready to move on to a new topic."

- The discussion is generating ideas and solutions. It isn't allowed to drift off on a tangent, and it's not just a gripe session.

- Everyone has an opportunity to contribute, but . . .
- No one is forced to speak if they prefer to listen.

As you well know from meetings you have attended, a good discussion can be a lively, productive learning experience. A rambling, nonfocused discussion is a waste of time. And a discussion that becomes argumentative or confrontational is just plain counterproductive.

In presenting a lecture, you are The Authority. But in a discussion session, you serve as facilitator, a role that connotes leadership but not power. You are responsible for maintaining the flow of ideas, in a friendly, comfortable atmosphere; for introducing topics that keep the group interested and involved; for keeping the ball rolling.

A discussion takes planning, even though it appears to be spontaneous. As the facilitator, you know what purpose the discussion will serve and what information you expect it to generate. You must research the subject as thoroughly as you would for a lecture—not to plan what you are going to say, but what question you are going to *ask*. You will not necessarily provide the solution to the problem, but you may suggest ways of approaching and analyzing it. If the group fails to raise some key points in the course of the discussion, you can fill in the gaps. And finally, it's your task to help the participants evaluate the ideas they have expressed and to draw conclusions. Some discussions are aimed at producing decisions and plans of action; others are simply intended to share knowledge. But all discussions should leave participants with the feeling that something has been accomplished.

USING QUESTIONS

As a workshop leader, you may never have all the right answers. But it's important to know all the right questions.

Like matchsticks, questions kindle the discussion. They may be used to arouse interest, gather data, or provide linkages from one topic to the next. They may be addressed to a specific individual or to the group in general.

Effective questions are:

Understandable

Provocative

Relevant

Interesting

Focused on one main thought

Briefly stated, in order to encourage equally concise, focused responses

The two basic types of questions are factual and open-ended. Factual questions have only one correct response. ("What day is today?" "What page are we on?") Factual questions can help you test the knowledge of the group or gain their attention. But the most useful questions for generating discussion are those that are open-ended, calling for feelings, ideas, and opinions.

Sometimes your questions will net a yes-or-no response. This is fine if you're looking for a consensus, but what if you want more information? If your question is only met with a flat *yes* or *no*, you can follow up with that provocative challenge, *Why?*

Here are nine ways to use questions, with examples of each.

Questions to Keep the Discussion Going

USES	EXAMPLES
Start the discussion.	"What is the biggest problem you have with your current staff?"
Arouse curiosity and interest.	"Do you know what a national survey found to be the three most common traits of good management?"
Gather new data.	"What are some disadvantages of offering work incentives?"
Help participants apply the information to their personal situation.	"Could you implement this policy without hiring more people?"
Arrive at a consensus.	"How many would agree with Joe's opinion?"
Get nonparticipants involved.	"Kathy, how would this affect you as a working mother?"
Keep the discussion on track.	"Good point. How does it relate to job turnover?"
Determine if the group understands the material.	"How many of you plan to try this procedure during the next fiscal year?"
Shift the discussion to new topic.	"Now that we've explored the problems, what are some possible solutions?"

A newsprint chart or blackboard can be a valuable aid in keeping the discussion focused and recording the conclusions that are reached. Obviously you don't want to write down everything that is said, or you'd be standing with your back to the group throughout the debate. However you may want to:

- Record new words or key points.
- Note names of authors, books, quotations—anything the group might want to remember for future reference.
- Draw charts, graphs, or other illustrations.
- List pros and cons, advantages and disadvantages, causes and cures, problems and solutions.

Finally, what about the questions the audience asks *you*? If you can dish it out, you should also be able to take it. In fact, you should welcome their questions. It's a sign that they are sincerely interested in the topic. It enables you to address their specific concerns instead of more general issues. And it gives you a chance to prove you can think on your feet.

Here are a few tips for fielding questions effectively in any group setting, whether it's an adult education workshop, a report to your company's board of directors, or a conference keynote address.

- Make sure everyone hears and understands the question. In a small group this is rarely a problem; but in a large group, you should repeat the question. This also gives you a chance to collect your thoughts before answering.
- Keep your answers brief and to the point. If you answer a question with a second speech, other members of the group will be reluctant to raise their concerns.
- Look directly at the person as he or she is asking the question, but address your answer to the entire audience.
- If you don't know an answer, say so. Don't be embarrassed or apologetic. If it's appropriate, offer to find out the information and get back to the questioner within a day or two.
- Don't allow yourself to be pulled into a personal discussion or argument. If the question would lead off on a tangent that does not concern the entire group, offer to speak with the individual privately, at the end of the program.

Most of the questions you'll encounter are straightforward and relevant, aimed at expanding upon or clarifying some previous point of discussion. But now and then, someone will raise an issue that is deliberately designed to put you on the defensive.

Cheerfully state your position, but don't let your interrogator goad you into a debate. The minute you start explaining yourself, you lose psychological ground. The best way to deflect a question that is meant to embarrass or harass is with humor. Failing that, say, "let's pursue that point together after the meeting." Never let someone engage you in an argument in public.

More Tips for Discussion Leaders

Follow a prepared agenda: an outline of topics to be discussed in a sensible order. This deters people from raising questions that will be answered later in the program.

Make sure everyone understands the issue being discussed and how it relates to the goals of the workshop.

Don't allow one or two talkative participants to dominate the discussion. Try to draw in quieter members of the audience. Encourage everyone to express a viewpoint.

Praise, accept, or acknowledge each person's contribution. *Never, ever* imply to a participant that his or her question is stupid or irrelevant (even if it is).

Don't be sarcastic.

Keep your questions clear, brief, and precise. A question that is too long and complex, or too general, is difficult to follow. If the group can't understand the question, they won't be able t) come up with any answers.

Don't ask leading questions, such as "Wouldn't you agree that . . ." A better phrasing is: "What would happen if . . ." or "What has been your experience?"

Avoid yes-and-no type questions, which tend to cut off discussion. Come prepared instead with inquiries that ask who, what, how, and why. These are more likely to provide real insights.

Call on people by name. There are two views on this. One recommends that the leader should address the person before phrasing the question, so he or she will have more time to prepare an answer. The other suggests posing the question to the entire group so that they are *all* considering an answer—then call on a specific individual.

Learn to "read" people: the furrowed brow that shows confusion or disagreement; the eager expression that indicates willingness to make a comment; the shuffling of feet or frequent whispering that signals loss of interest.

Confine the discussion to a relatively short time frame. Five or 10 minutes on one issue is generally adequate. If the remarks become rambling or repetitious, move on to the next topic.

Avoid mechanical transitions. ("My next question is . . .") Try to use a participant's comment to lead into the next question.

Summarize or reemphasize key points and conclusions before moving on to the next topic.

Finally, how do you keep a lively interchange going? Here are eight ways to respond to a participant's comment besides saying "Yes!," "Right!," and nodding your head:

1. Elaborate on the participant's remark by adding your own opinion.
2. Paraphrase it in your own words.
3. Generalize from it. Show how it applies in a broader context.
4. Integrate it with previous topics or participants' comments.
5. Praise it for its insight and relevance.
6. Disagree with it, if that is your inclination. But don't evaluate who's right and who's wrong.
7. Summarize it, especially if the comment was somewhat long and rambling.
8. Bridge it to the next point you planned to make. Or use it as a transition to a fresh topic.

Chapter Seven

Getting Participants Involved

We are attending a seminar called "Lecture and Discussion Management." And if that sounds dry and scholarly, you haven't met Dean N. Osterman, Ph.D., director of instructional and faculty development at Oregon State University. He is here to show participants specific techniques to:

- Turn dull lectures into lively, organized learning experiences.
- Use questions to spark interest, hold attention, and double-check understanding.
- Avoid lecturing "at" people and get them more involved in discussions.

This is not a three-piece-suit crowd gathered for the seminar. Most of the participants are college faculty and graduate students wishing to improve their teaching skills. Osterman is dressed in tone with the audience, in a plaid sport shirt and leather vest. Like the host of a dinner party, he greets people as they come through the door, shaking hands and committing their first names to memory. He introduces us to one another. There's a table spread with bowls of raisins and peanuts, hot coffee, and a jug of apple cider. The atmosphere is already warm and comfortable. This is going to be fun.

Indeed, that's right up there on the list of workshop objectives printed across the first page of the flipchart:

1. Identify problems with establishing a discussion
2. To view and try a few solutions

3. To practice and try microteaching

4. To have some fun

We are now seated in a semicircle, telling our names, what we teach, why we came. Osterman dislikes tables. They create barriers between him and his audience. So do straight rows of chairs that bank people in columns behind one another. "By the way, Dean is my *name*," he grins, sheepishly relating an incident when he was accorded red carpet treatment because his name was mistaken for his position. What he means is: "I'm just like you people. I have no pretensions of high authority." He briefly describes his own teaching experience to establish a common bond.

At this point, Osterman could step up to the lectern and begin describing the typical problems that teachers experience in engaging their students in discussions. He knows what the problems are. Instead, he batches us in groups of three to discuss the problems *we* most often experience. He hands a person in each triad a different colored felt-tip marker and asks us to write our three most persistent problems on the flipchart.

Now we have three pages of newsprint and a long, colorful list of problems:

- Eager beavers. The people who always answer first.
- Participants who are shy and difficult to draw out.
- Discussions that trail off on a tangent.
- Side conversations between pairs of participants, distracting you and the rest of the class.
- Ramblers. People who gain the floor and then go on and on about personal issues that are not relevant.

. . . And so on.

"We'll be addressing these specific situations," Osterman promises. "First, I want to give you an overview of the four different types of students you will have in your classroom and the different ways in which they learn." (Osterman's four categories of learners are described in Chapter Four of this book). He illustrates his lecture with cartoons and other images on the overhead projector. One drawing shows two people trying to shove a large round elephant through a small square barn door. "How does this relate to teaching?" he asks rhetorically. We can all see the analogy of the hapless teacher trying to ramrod information through to an unreceptive student. Throughout this lesson, Osterman solicits response from the group.

By now about 75 minutes have passed since the workshop

began. We have already done two large group-brainstorming sessions, a couple of two- and three-person buzz groups, a written exercise in the workbook, and heard a 20-minute informational lecture. One more change of pace: He takes us through a quick review of the workbook materials and then calls for a seven-minute break.

MOTIVATING STUDENTS TO LEARN

We reconvene, having stretched our legs and refilled our coffee cups. At the beginning of any workshop, there's a sense of anticipation, even tension, that comes from not knowing what to expect, or what will be expected from you. That's gone now. Everyone feels relaxed and on top of things. Our leader, meanwhile, is in the process of placing an empty bottle on a stool and a funnel on top of the bottle. Ah, we see what he's up to. He is going to illustrate how a teacher pours water (information) into an empty container (the student).

Splash! Osterman has just *thrown* the water from the pitcher from a distance five feet away. The rug, the stool, and a few astonished people are wet, but the bottle is empty.

"When you're teaching, you have to target your information to the audience," he explains, grinning impishly.

"Pouring can be compared to teaching," he continues, now aiming the rest of the water directly through the funnel. "The first step, of course, is getting the cap off the bottle. This can be achieved by getting the students *ready to learn*. What are some ways to achieve readiness?" The ball is back in our court. The group suggests the following:

HOW TO GET STUDENTS READY TO LEARN

- Present an overview. Outline what the course will cover so that participants can anticipate what they will learn.
- Convey enthusiasm. Share the reasons why you believe the subject is important.
- Arouse curiosity. Raise questions about your subject that will pique students' interest.
- Show relevance. Make them see that your information has practical applications and can help them solve problems.
- Use humor. It gets people's attention and builds rapport.

"That's only five ways," Osterman goads us, writing each on the blackboard. "I've never had a group come up with six. I wonder why no one can ever come up with *six*?" Finally we catch on, and someone supplies the sixth tactic for creating learning readiness.

- *Challenge* the students.

After readiness is achieved, the next step is pouring the information, without spilling or overflowing. What are some ways of achieving this? Another brainstorming session follows, and the group comes up with this list:

HOW TO PRESENT MATERIAL EFFECTIVELY

- Subdivide it. Organize and present the material in bits and pieces instead of in one lump. Providing a course outline or workshop agenda helps here.
- Modify it. Tailor your information to your audience. Two communication-skills workshops may contain many of the same basic concepts, but one directed at high-level managers will be much different from one conducted for a group of hospital aides.
- Illustrate it. "Audiovisual ideas serve the same function as funnels," Osterman contends. "They focus the information more clearly, as a lens channels a beam of light. They should *supplement* the instruction, not *be* the instruction," he adds.
- Relate it. Continue to stress the applicability of your subject matter to real-life issues. In other words:
- Translate it: from the general to the specific.

As water evaporates from a bottle, so will learning fade after the course or workshop is finished. How do you help students retain what you've taught them? How to put a stopper on the bottle?

HOW TO IMPROVE LEARNING RETENTION

- Repeat it. Bring up the key points of your presentation more than once, within several contexts.
- Integrate it. Take a previous concept and link it with a new concept so that students will see a pattern.
- Summarize the key points. Or have the students summarize what they have learned.
- Encourage them to *apply* what they have learned. Perhaps they can do this during class, through role play or fill-in-the-blank exercise sheets.
- Provide handout materials. Take-home exercises and a course summary will help the students review the information whenever necessary and refresh their memories.

TALKING IT OVER

For the past half-hour Osterman could have stood before us and, in an authoritative, precise manner, outlined all of the preceding points on preparation, presentation, and retention. It would have been faster than soliciting the answers from us. But would it have been more efficient? Not necessarily.

"Your objective as a workshop leader is to team what you know with what the audience knows. Match your information to their needs," he states. "Do you want a formula? It's simple: A workshop is 50 percent your knowledge, ideas, organization, efforts, and presentation and 50 percent ideas, questions, curiosity, and suggestions from the audience."

The discussion method Dean Osterman advocates is not a free-form debate or bull session. You, the leader, have clearly in mind what you want your students to learn. You know the main points that should be raised on any list-building or information-assembling exercise you conduct. You know the solution, conclusion, ideas, or attitudes you want them to reach in the end. But you let *them* come up with these answers.

"Using the discussion method for teaching purposes is much different than using it in the context of a group-brainstorming or consciousness-raising session," he emphasizes. "It is highly focused. You have a predetermined outcome, but you let it evolve through the participants. Consequently, they feel more competent."

People tend to remember information much better if they raise issues and develop examples from their own experience rather than if the leader merely spoon-feeds facts to them, he explains. They are more likely to apply the solutions if they find them personally relevant.

During this talk on discussion management, Osterman takes an apple out of his bag of tricks and tosses it into the audience. A young man with quick reflexes catches it and tosses it back. Osterman aims the apple at another participant, who then bats it sideways to another member of the group. What is happening here?

The apple—or it could be a rubber ball—represents the discussion topic. When the ball is bouncing back and forth between the leader and individual participants, the leader has control of the discussion. When it is tossed around among members of the group, the discussion becomes free-form, less tightly controlled. There is no telling what direction it may be headed. Should the leader try to regain control of the ball (i.e., discussion)? That depends—upon whether the debate appears to be meaningful and constructive or seems to be going off on a tangent.

"The instructor remains the gatekeeper of the discussion," Osterman states. "Instructors can either inhibit or encourage the open exchange of ideas. How might they hinder it? One way is by answering their own questions before anyone else has the opportunity!"

Instructors must avoid dominating the discussion, and they must guard against letting one or two talkative participants monopolize it as well. Solicit contributions from other members. ("Who *else* has had this experience?") Call for a consensus. ("How many of you would agree with Joe's opinion?")

It's clear that Dean Osterman practices what he preaches. He has definite biases in favor of the discussion method of teaching. The traditional lecture has its place, but it can be far more effective if it is accompanied by well-designed, deliberate questions that produce involvement and feedback. But he didn't just tell us so. He let us discover it for ourselves, through the same process.

In conclusion, the group came up with these major advantages to the discussion method:

- It's spontaneous and unpredictable—and thus holds people's attention.
- It helps the leader discover any misunderstandings and clarify the subject.
- It personalizes the information for individual participants.
- It may turn up new knowledge, examples, or anecdotes that leaders can add to their own store of material.

"Teaching a class or conducting a workshop, you realize that your students are a fantastic resource," Osterman believes. "That assembled group probably knows, collectively, far more than you do. One of your greatest challenges is to draw out that collective energy and expertise. That is what makes for a dynamic, mutually rewarding learning experience."

Chapter Eight

Places, Spaces, Props, and Plugs

It's not just what you say but *how* you say it. And *when* and *where* you say it counts as well.

Every workshop, no matter how universal its subject matter, must be shaped and modified to suit the needs of the audience. A group's age range, male/female ratio, educational backgrounds, occupation, political orientation, all affect your presentation style and content.

In particular, you need to know how much knowledge and experience they already have in your subject—in other words, where they're coming from and what they're expecting.

One factor that influences participants' expectations and attendance is timing.

WHEN WILL IT TAKE PLACE?

There are several time frames to consider when planning a presentation:

The time of year.   The best months to schedule workshops seem to be the following months: mid-September through mid-November (fall still means "back-to-learning" to most adults, a carry-over from childhood); January through March (a change of pace for the winter doldrums); April and early May (spring brings a sense of renewal). The summer months are suited only for outdoor recreation workshops. Do not even consider December or August.

Regional factors may affect your seasonal choices. In the northern states, a program in January or February could be wiped out by a winter snowstorm. Other parts of the country are vulnerable to long rainy seasons or hot, humid spells. If you're planning a workshop in an unfamiliar city, consult the local chamber of commerce about weather conditions. Also, inquire about special community events (harvest festivals, sports tournaments) that might overbook local hotels. And especially steer clear of all national and religious holidays, election days, high school and college graduations, and the World Series.

The day of week. The best days of the week for a business or professional program are Wednesday, Thursday, and Tuesday, in that order. Most people seem to need the beginning of the week to get organized and Fridays to catch up. Mid-week evenings and Saturdays are best for non-company-sponsored programs that people attend at their own expense.

The time of day. An audience's expectations and attentiveness may vary significantly with the time of day you are scheduled to speak. For example:

After breakfast: Morning audiences are alert, anticipative. Having invested a chunk of productive time away from the office, they expect serious, substantive information.

After lunch: See those somewhat glazed expressions? Many people experience a mid-day energy slump, so avoid films or slide presentations that encourage drowsiness. Plan some participatory activities instead.

After dinner: Audiences who have just enjoyed a couple of drinks and a meal—or perhaps, a banquet—expect a program in keeping with the festive mood. You'll win points by keeping it light, entertaining, and above all, short.

WHERE TO HOLD THE PROGRAM

The program is ready and the dates are set. Where is the best place to hold it? Location and facilities are important. You might make two almost identical presentations to two similar audiences, but the mood in a posh restaurant will be quite different than in a high school cafeteria.

An attractive, reputable meeting place reflects the quality of your program. High quality often draws higher attendance. Comfortable chairs, strategically arranged, make people relaxed and ready to learn. Some general considerations about facilities and room setups will set the stage for the later sections of this chapter on visual aids, props, and electrical outlets.

If you are engaged to conduct a workshop for a business or professional organization, or as part of a conference, most of the decisions about facilities will be made by your sponsors. Most large companies have their own meeting rooms. Conference organizers will have already booked hotel space for their event.

But what if you are mounting the seminar independently or working through an adult education network that allows you to select your own facilities? Many options are open to you. Be sure to take the following factors into consideration:

Convenience.　　Obviously, you should choose a meeting site that is close as possible to your prospective audience. If the workshop is aimed at local residents, select a well-known, centrally located facility close to a main thoroughfare. Don't limit yourself to hotels. A library, church, neighborhood center, or other community building might provide good accommodations at a much lower cost.

If you are hoping to attract out-of-town participants, your first choice might be a hotel on the outskirts of town or perhaps near the airport, so it is accessible from the expressway. Make sure it has a prominent billboard, easy to spot from a moving automobile.

Whatever facility you choose, it should be close to a known street or landmark, so that you can give simple directions to the site by telephone. And make sure it has access to plenty of parking.

Atmosphere.　　Before you commit yourself to any meeting space, check it out in person. Is it the right size for the number of people you expect? Is there a thermostat in the room so that you can adjust the temperature? How about ventilation and lighting? A dim or stuffy room will put your audience to sleep. Windows will help the air circulation, but make sure they are properly shaded if your program is scheduled in the daytime and you plan to show slides or film.

Acoustics.　　While you're looking at prospective meeting sites, listen as well. Can you hear traffic from the street outside? Clanking dishes from the kitchen? Is the room located down an isolated corridor or surrounded by other meeting places? Many hotels and conference facilities feature large rooms with movable walls. This setup is flexible but not necessarily soundproof. Before contracting for any space, try to obtain assurances that nothing boisterous will be going on above, below, or next door. Jeanne Paul, who had agreed to conduct an all-day writers' workshop for a community center, was not too concerned when she learned that a wedding reception was slated for the same facility. The reception turned out to be in an adjacent room and featured a live dance band!

Comfort. Ventilation, visibility, and freedom from distracting noises are all essential to a good learning atmosphere. But don't overlook the smaller sources of convenience and comfort: ample parking, clean restrooms, drinking fountains, coat racks. The checklist provided in Appendix A will cue you on what to look for.

Class. The facility you select is one of the measures by which people will judge your program. First impressions count. If the Main Street Hotel has a reputation for high quality and service, and people read in your brochure that your seminar will be held there, they will associate quality and competence with you as well. High expectations are likely to lead to high enrollment.

Notice that "quality" is not synonymous with "expensive." Some hotels charge higher room fees because they provide extras that aren't important to you. Unless participants are checking in for the night, they aren't likely to care that the place has an indoor swimming pool.

The best surroundings will never disguise an inferior program. But a shabby or uncomfortable room will greatly detract from an excellent program. Long after they've forgotten your "five rules of closing sales," participants will remember the cigarette burns on the tablecloth, the crazy air conditioner that plunged temperatures to 55 degrees.

People can't learn what they can't see or hear clearly. Cheap or even free space is not a bargain if it inhibits the learning process. Invest in quality and you will build credibility—and that leads to profit in the long run.

EVERYONE, PLEASE BE SEATED

Whether your program is held in a living room or a lecture hall, one factor in its success will be the way people are seated. Just like furniture in a home, chairs in a meeting room convey different degrees of formality and friendliness. To a surprising extent, seating arrangements can either encourage or hinder the group's willingness to ask questions or join in discussion.

Straight lines convey more formality, even rigidity. Columns of desks or chairs harken back to high school, a place many adults associate with unpleasant, authoritarian learning experiences. For this reason, many workshop leaders prefer more informal room setups, arranging chairs in a crescent or horseshoe. Circles seem to work better than lines to promote a relaxed atmosphere and group participation.

Some seating arrangements will be dictated by the size of the group and the type of program. If your audience numbers more than 100, you are usually limited to lecture-style seating. If you're making a presentation following dinner, the audience will already be seated around tables. Here are some of the various kinds of seating arrangements you may create or encounter, with some advantages and disadvantages of each.

Conference table.   The smallest groups—about 8 to 12 people—can be seated around an oblong conference table with you at the helm. (Chairs should be placed 30 to 36 inches apart for any of the chair/table arrangements on this list.)

Horseshoe.   By placing six or eight oblong tables end-to-end in a U-shape, you can enlarge the conference table plan to accommodate more people. A favored arrangement by many workshop leaders, the horseshoe is flexible, informal, and intimate. Each person has a writing surface and good eye contact. A "closed horseshoe" (i.e., a square) seats a few more people and emphasizes the equal status of all participants. The horseshoe is a good choice for groups of up to 26 people.

Classroom.   By positioning the oblong tables in double rows, with all chairs facing the front of the room, you create a more traditional schoolroom atmosphere. The climate is a bit more serious and academic—better suited to programs that emphasize listening more than discussing. Again be aware, however, that not all adults remember their school days with nostalgia. They may learn more willingly and readily in a less formal environment.

Banquet style.   Many workshops take place in restaurants or hotels where the meeting rooms are set up with round tables, each seating about eight people. This can be conducive to a good learning climate, since the audience is already seated in circles.

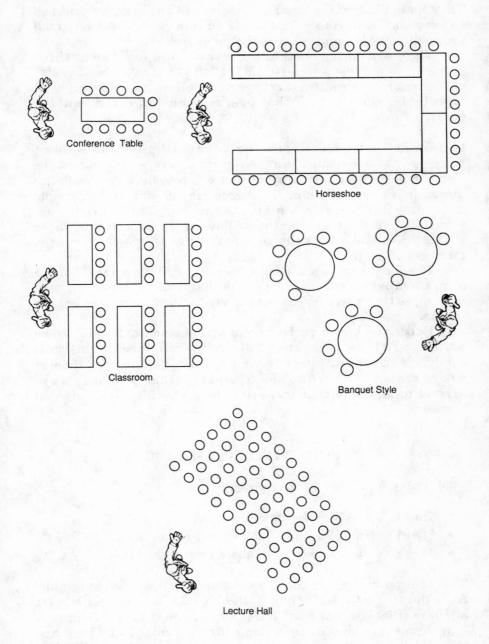

Conference Table

Horseshoe

Classroom

Banquet Style

Lecture Hall

They have likely introduced themselves to one another and feel relaxed and comfortable. The situation is made-to-order for small group discussions and other learning exercises.

The disadvantage is that if the tables are full, two or three people have to twist around in their chairs to see you. So if you're planning on this seating arrangement, allow for five people at each table, not eight, so that everyone has an equal vantage point.

Lecture hall. If you're speaking before a large group—40 or more—you may have to resort to rows of chairs, auditorium style. You can soften the formality of this setup by having the chairs placed in a crescent shape, or stagger the chairs so that people are not seated directly behind one another. This will also improve visibility and eye contact. Allow wide aisles so that those sitting in the middle of the row don't have to crawl over large numbers of people.

The ideal chairs are desk type with writing arms. If these aren't available, you might provide handout folders with stiff backing so that participants have a writing surface for easier note taking.

Experiment with various room arrangements. People can be seated in T-shapes, V-shapes, full circles—whatever seems most conducive to the learning experience. Unless you're in a theater where seats are bolted to the floor, encourage people to move around in any way that increases their visibility and personal comfort.

SEEING IS UNDERSTANDING

Visual aids serve several purposes:

- They help people follow ideas in sequence.
- They illustrate and help emphasize key concepts.
- They give the audience something to look at besides you.

This section will cover the most commonly used teaching aids, from the simple to the sophisticated. You're familiar with most of these. Blackboards and chalk, for example, do not require a lengthy description or operating instructions. But there are things you may want to know about visual-aid equipment before incorporating them into your workshop.

One general observation: You can invest lots of money in custom-designed slides and videotapes, but don't necessarily presume they are more effective than grease pencils and newsprint. The best visuals are often the most simple devices. They should enhance your presentation, not upstage it.

My bias is toward blackboards and flipcharts—in other words: low tech. They can't break down in the middle of your program. They don't require electrical outlets or extension cords. The fewer *things* you have to rely on in your workshop—especially mechanical things—the less there is to go wrong.

Chalkboards. Some instructors disparage chalkboards as being messy and childish, making adults feel like they're back in grade school. But many workshops are held in high school or college classrooms, where chalkboards are built in, usually five feet high and stretching the length of two walls. What a resource! And it's already there. You don't have to haul it back and forth with you.

But do bring your own chalk and eraser. I have taught workshops in dozens of classroom facilities and, invariably, the chalk trays are empty. On a good night, you might find one chalk piece the size of a corn kernel.

Hotels and conference centers can usually provide large portable chalkboards, but check out the room lighting before opting for this. The glare sometimes makes the board impossible to read from some angles. A newsprint pad might better serve your purpose.

One more thing: Remember that chalkboards produce chalk dust. If you're using a chalkboard, never wear a dark suit.

Newsprint pad. This is a cheap, basic tool for fostering group involvement. At the beginning of the workshop, you can ask participants what issues they wish to address. Writing them on the pad with a felt-tip marker or grease pencil, you create an agenda for the program. Later, you can distribute markers and sheets of newsprint to tables during small group discussions. The participants can record their conclusions in large print and tape them to the wall for the reaction of the full group. Participants can continue to refer to these notations throughout the program since, unlike the blackboard, they won't get erased.

Newsprint pads measure 24 by 36 inches, come in 50 and 100 sheet sizes, and are available at most art- and office-supply stores. You'll need an easel to support your pad—most hotels can provide you with one, and often the pad as well—and plenty of masking tape.

Flipchart. Another inexpensive, versatile, and very effective teaching aid is a 24- by 36-inch pad on which you have already printed the key points of your lecture. As you turn the pages, the words and graphics cue you to the topics you wish to discuss, in proper sequence. It serves as a script for your presentation.

You can use a newsprint pad for this purpose, but a pad of higher-quality, heavier weight art paper will better withstand repeated use. This can also be ordered through office- or art-supply stores, and is available plain, lined, or with a grid. After you've prepared the flipchart, bolt it to a piece of illustration board or Fome-Cor (a stiff, lightweight backing sold by art-supply stores and frame shops). The chart can now be propped up on your easel.

Easel. Hotels and conference centers usually provide speakers with easels, but you can never be sure if their model will be the right size for your flipchart. And on many occasions, you may be speaking in facilities like schools or churches that don't have these resources. This means you'll have to prop your chart on a high-backed chair and hold it awkwardly in place for the duration of the workshop.

If your program often involves the use of a newsprint pad or flipchart, buy your own easel. For about $60 you can own one that's lightweight, portable, collapsible, affordable, and, most of all, dependable.

Flannel board. You can create your own self-adhering bulletin board by stretching a piece of flannel material over a piece of Fome-Cor or a large wood or metal frame. Strips of words, sentences, or pictures backed with felt, flannel, or light sandpaper will stick to the flannel board, and so will Styrofoam cutouts. Flannel is available at any fabric store, and a frame can be easily constructed of plywood.

The advantage of the flannel board is that it allows you to present a sequence of ideas, one step at a time. You can move the ideas around to change the rank order of priorities or introduce new concepts.

SOME DESIGN GUIDELINES

In designing visuals, whether for newsprint pad, flipchart, or overhead transparency:

Keep it simple.
Never exceed eight lines on the page.
Never exceed 25 characters across, including spaces.
Never put more than three curves on a graph. One or two are better.
Use key words or phrases, not complete sentences.
Black markers are easiest to read, with colors for highlights.
Simple graphics add interest.

But aim for readability, not grand artistry. Block letters, not Old English script, is in order here.
Remember, you are not designing a circus poster.

Overhead transparencies. Flannel boards, chalkboards, and flipcharts fall into the category of "intimate" visual aids. For large audiences, an overhead projector will enable you to flash your message across a big screen. You can assemble a large stock of transparencies, including words, graphs, cartoons, and other illustrations, and arrange them to suit your individual audience. There are several special features to this device. It projects over the shoulder, so that you can operate it while facing the audience. The images can be seen without darkening the room. And using a special pencil, you can draw on the transparencies as they are being projected, underlining a phrase or circling a correct answer. You can also overlay one transparency on top of another to illustrate growth or progress. Transparencies can be prepared for you commercially, or you can purchase the special paper and make your own.

An opaque projector, similar to the overhead, can be used to show items that have not been transferred to transparencies. Using lights and mirrors, this device can project pages of books, photographs, printing, and drawings on opaque paper. The opaque projector does require a darkened room, however, and the screen images are usually not as clearly visible as those shown with transparencies.

Overhead and opaque projectors can be rented, but they are often provided without charge by restaurants and conference facilities.

Slides and filmstrips.   Sometimes a picture is really worth a thousand words. If your subject is, say, French Impressionist painting, a phrase on a flipchart is inadequate. Only the image of the art work, in full color, can bring it to life.

Slides can also be created from printed material like graphs and texts, but they may not enhance your presentation. Fred Steingold, an attorney and lecturer, relates this incident:

> One of the worst seminars I've ever attended was put on by an accounting firm, ostensibly to enlighten lawyers about tax reform. Immediately after the introduction, the room was plunged into total darkness. For the next hour, we were treated to a series of slides, expensively produced for this session.
>
> Words flashed across the screen while the speaker read from a prepared text. The speaker made references to section such-and-such from the Federal Tax Code, apparently assuming we knew from memory what he was talking about. He failed to recognize that this audience came specifically because we were *not* highly informed about federal tax matters. Why else would we have attended?
>
> However, in a pitch dark room, no one could even take notes or ask questions!

Steingold's experience illustrates the surprising fact that expensive, overdone visual aids may actually alienate your audience instead of impressing them. In a dark meeting room, slides can distance the participants from one another and stop conversation cold. They can put people to sleep!

So, use slides only if your audience is too large and your subject matter too visual for simpler choices. Then, select only the best specimens, and arrange them so that the presentation keeps pace with your commentary. Plan for each slide to show about 15 to 20 seconds on the screen. Practice and practice. Upside-down slides are amusing in your living room, but not in a professional seminar.

Films and videotapes.   A good, relevant film or videotape can provide a welcome change of pace, particularly during an all-day conference or workshop. Your local library or college extension service probably offers a full catalogue of educational films that can be rented (along with a projector) at reasonable cost. Allow time to preview the film or tape before incorporating it in your program.

And don't just spring a film or tape on the audience. Prepare them for what they'll be watching; alert them what to look for and explain why it is pertinent to the subject. Afterwards, allow time for the viewers to talk about it. Short (three- to five-minute) productions called "trigger tapes" are especially designed to raise participants' consciousness and promote discussion.

Videotape equipment. Lights, camera, action! Here we're not just referring to *showing* a videotape, but producing it as well. Workshop participants are taped in the act of performing some activity or learning a new skill. Then, through instant replay, they get to "see themselves as others see them." The showing is often followed by a group critique.

Videotape equipment is a particularly valuable tool in communications workshops—a category that includes teaching, negotiating, public speaking, and other presentation skills. When people see themselves on tape, they can readily assess their strengths and weaknesses in such areas as hand gestures and eye contact. Another advantage is that videotape, used this way, is very involving. It is not a passive learning experience.

A BAG OF TRICKS

Diane Ciampa is beginning her workshop on stress management by slowly pouring water over the top of a large sponge. "Your alarm fails to go off." Drip. "Your kids are bickering at each other over the breakfast table." Splat. "You're caught in a traffic snarl and late to work." Splat. "A customer calls and complains to you about an order that's late." Splat. Splop. The sponge absorbs all it can take and then finally, the water seeps through and drips onto the floor.

Ciampa could have just said, "Lots of little pressures and problems tax our ability to withstand stress." But the sponge created a visual image that everyone in the audience could understand instantly.

Simple props can be used very effectively to illustrate a point, capture attention, and connect with the audience. The best ones may be familiar household objects—an egg timer, a piggy bank, a set of keys. But a prop's relevance to your subject should be readily obvious—never gimmicky or contrived. If its place in your presentation seems strained, drop it. Let the audience reaction be your guide.

Of course, props are not optional in demonstration-type seminars. If you're teaching about plant propagation, you'll need gardening tools, potting soil, fertilizer, seedlings—the works. A prop for a course in auto mechanics might include an entire car.

Finally, here's a category of props you may not have considered: people. When Tavi Fulkerson conducts workshops on "Dressing for a Professional Image," she uses live models and members of the audience to demonstrate her comments about color and style.

Lecterns. While we're on the subject of props, do you really need a lectern? Some speakers seem to use them, literally, to prop themselves up. I recall one clubwoman who, obviously nervous, stood frozen behind a lectern and gripped its sides as if she were hanging onto a life raft. She had the appearance of a suspended talking head.

You may be able to hide behind a lectern while giving an after-dinner speech, but during a workshop you need to be mobile. Plant your notes on it, if necessary, and then move the lectern off to the side. You should be the focal point of the presentation, not some stick of furniture.

Microphones. Like many pieces of electronic equipment, microphones can be intimidating. They squawk and hum. The volume needs adjusting. Your voice fades in and out if you don't keep your lips in position. By the time you've figured out how to use it effectively, your lecture is finished.

My most memorable experience with a microphone occurred when I was asked to present one of three concurrent seminars at a state realtors convention. The programs were all being held in the hotel's grand ballroom, which was divided into three meeting rooms by movable, soundproof walls. About 80 people were gathered at each session.

As I opened my mouth to speak, a loud male voice boomed out of my microphone. The voice of the speaker in the adjacent room was feeding through my mike, loud and clear. Apparently all three speaker systems had been interconnected during the previous session, which had been attended by the full delegation.

The experience reaffirmed three basic precepts about the seminar business:

- Expect the unexpected.
- Never lose your sense of humor.
- Avoid using a microphone unless the size of the group makes it mandatory. Learn to project your voice instead.

Name tags. Name tags are extremely helpful in creating a friendly, personable learning climate. They enable you to address people by name instead of by "you there," and they help the participants get to know one another. Having preprinted name tags ready for participants at the registration table issues a note of welcome. Be sure to use large lettering that can be read from a distance.

Name Card

Name cards. If participants are seated at tables, provide them with sheets of stiff paper, folded lengthwise, and felt-tip markers. They should write their names and, optionally, their job title and organization on both sides so that it can be read by both you and members of the group seated behind them. A 9- by 12-inch manila file folder, cut in half, works fine for this.

Quizzes and questionnaires. Short written exercises provide a good change of pace from the highly verbal lecture/discussion format. They give participants a chance to process what has been said, to turn their thoughts inward and see how the topic applies to them.

A test can be designed to measure knowledge, skills, attitudes, or experience. But perhaps its most important result is that it increases the participant's self-awareness.

While most written exercises are intended for the students' benefit, they may also be designed to help you know more about them and better meet their needs. For example, at the beginning of your course or workshop, you can distribute sheets of paper and ask each person to answer the following questions:

1. What are the main problems you have with (workshop issue) at the moment?

2. What do you most hope to gain from this learning experience?

Handout materials.   There's no rule that says a workshop has to provide handout materials. And that's why yours should. People like getting something extra and unexpected. But besides earning appreciation, handout materials benefit you, the teacher, as well. They build flexibility into your lecture by providing you a fallback. If you run short of time and have to skim one or two subjects, you can tell the group, "that's covered more thoroughly in the handout materials."

Handout materials may include:

- Questionnaires, tests, and other written exercises.
- Summary sheets you prepared yourself.
- Reprints of articles or book chapters that are relevant to your program. (Be sure to obtain copyright permission.)
- A list of resources—local persons, organizations, or supply sources participants can draw upon.
- A roster of participants' names and addresses, in case they want to stay in contact with each other.
- A bibliography.
- An evaluation sheet.

An effective workshop always leaves participants wishing for more. Handout materials supply that extra information and the means of pursuing the topic further on their own.

Handouts also give people something to remember you by, so make sure they are prominently inscribed with your name, business, and phone number. They may want to recommend your program to others.

Chapter Nine

Getting Off to the Right Start

You're invited to a classy dinner party. Pleased, you promptly notify the hosts of your acceptance. On the appointed day, you get dressed up, wrap up a bottle of wine, and arrive on time. With a sense of high anticipation, you ring the bell.

A child answers the door. "Mom's in the shower and Dad just went out to buy ice," he explains, ushering you into a disheveled living room. Newspapers are strewn about the couch. Some other guests whom you don't know are standing around awkwardly. You think you smell something burning in the kitchen.

Conducting a workshop is like giving a party. From the first, you want your guests, the participants, to feel welcome and comfortable. You do this by creating an atmosphere that says, "I'm ready and waiting for you!" not, "Omigod, is it *that* time already?"

Let's replay the dinner party scene like this: Your hosts greet you at the door. They take your coat, offer you something to drink, and introduce you to the other guests. The table in the dining room is set. There's soft music on the stereo. People are relaxed, talking easily. This time, you're glad you came.

You can create the same atmosphere of warmth and readiness in a classroom or community meeting room. All it takes is the same attention to details, and allowing yourself enough time to look after those details. That's why, the first rule of training is ...

Arrive early. This doesn't mean 5 or 10 minutes before your workshop participants start showing up. Allow at least 20 minutes if someone else is sponsoring your presentation (and taking care of matters such as registration and room preparations). Allow 45 minutes to an hour if you're handling these logistics yourself.

Why? Because even the most reputable, high-priced hotel may not provide everything exactly as you requested. Instructions can get garbled. You asked for a movie screen, and they delivered a blackboard. You ordered coffee and Danish, and they produced setups for a bar.

See Appendix A for a complete list of everything you need to check for your workshop—equipment, supplies, and meeting space. Here are some things you should check immediately upon arrival:

Lobby signs.   Make sure the title, time, and location of your program is correctly listed on the hotel's announcement board. (Make sure it is even listed in the first place.) If you're meeting in some other type of facility that does not provide a specific space for announcements, bring your own sign. In fact, bring several signs with directional arrows to point the way to your meeting room. Make it easy for people to find you.

First impressions count. Professionally lettered signs on heavy card stock with your company name and logo will cast a more favorable image than the word "workshop" and an arrow, scrawled in pen on looseleaf paper.

Room setup.   Now that people can find you, make sure the room looks presentable. Are the tables and chairs arranged as you requested? (It's not unusual to find them scattered about at random or stacked against the wall!) Allow plenty of time to put the room in order. Also allow time to find a maintenance person to help you.

Registration table.   If an outside organization is sponsoring your workshop, its staff will see to registrations. But if you're putting it on, you'll want to position a table at the meeting room entrance, ready to check in the arrivals. The table should be equipped with:

> List of expected participants
>
> Name tags, preprinted with the names of persons who registered in advance
>
> Additional name tags for persons who register at the door
>
> Felt-tip markers and extra pens

Receipts

Folders with handout materials

Extra copies of your brochure for this or future programs (in case participants want to pass one on to a friend)

Atmosphere. The room that you have been assigned may have been unused and sealed off for the past week. Consequently, it may take some time to get it warmed up (or cooled down) to a comfortable temperature. It may have last been used by a group of cigar-smoking conventioneers. Arrive early enough to air out the room, adjust the temperature, or—if the conditions are sufficiently uncomfortable to warrant it—request a change to a different room altogether.

Coffee and other refreshments. The coffee should be ready and waiting when participants begin to arrive. There's no point in having it wheeled in just as you begin the introductions. On the other hand, you don't want it to be prepared so far in advance that it pours like catsup. Taste it. If it's bitter, insist on a fresh pot.

Doughnuts or pastries will endear you to most participants, (unless you are conducting a weight-loss seminar). Pitchers of fruit juice are also welcome. But keep within a reasonable budget. Most participants recognize that the extra cost was figured into the workshop fee.

Remember that some people prefer decaffeinated coffee or hot tea. Be sure to provide hot water and tea bags and packets of instant decaffeinated—or a pot of brewed decaffeinated if it's available.

Of course, some people would prefer a chocolate malt or a can of beer. Realize that you can't accommodate everyone.

AND NOW . . . ON WITH THE SHOW!

"Setting the right learning climate" doesn't mean adjusting the room temperature.

It refers to the warmth you project as people arrive, and that you maintain right on through the workshop. A smile, a handshake, that first exchange of comments will go far to alleviate your own anxiety and put your workshop participants at ease as well.

The opening minutes of your seminar are crucial to creating the kind of relaxed, informal atmosphere that is most conducive to adult learning. This is the time when you:

- *Establish your humanness.* Tell the group a little—take one minute, maximum—about your job, your personal background, and what brought you to the business of teaching workshops. ("I became interested in time management out of desperation, trying, like many of you, to find a system for juggling a job, a home, a family, and a two-week backup of laundry.")

- *Get acquainted with the participants.* Do this either through a round of introductions (if it is a small group of 20 or so) or some show-of-hands questions ("How many of you are here today because you've recently taken on new marketing responsibilities in your company?").

- *Get a sense of their expectations*—and outline what you hope to accomplish during the session.

- *Take care of housekeeping matters.* Advise them where the restrooms are located, whether smoking is permitted, and what time you'll be taking a break.

William A. Draves, national director of the Learning Resources Network, puts it well:

> Students want to know you are their 'superior' in the subject about which they are to learn, but they also want to know that you are a peer in every other way. Distance, becoming an authority figure, or aloofness do not enhance adult learning. So you also want to establish a relationship with your participants that indicates some of your personal, though not necessarily private characteristics.[1]

Professional trainer and consultant Kenneth W. Jones believes it's also useful to start off with a disclaimer. "Many people come to workshops with unrealistic expectations. So I remind them: A trainer is not a magician, who can change their environment, or a therapist, who can solve all their personal problems. There are no easy cookbook recipes for achieving the changes they are seeking," he stresses.

"It's easy enough to attend a workshop and even to take notes. But in the end, it's up to them to take action." This puts the responsibility for learning squarely on the shoulders of the participants, Jones says, although it doesn't relieve you of yours. You still have to put the ideas across and instill motivation.

Introductions—or an open discussion of "What brings you to this class? What are you hoping to learn?"—can serve as a good

---

[1]William A. Draves, *How To Teach Adults* (Manhattan, Kan.: The Learning Resources Network, 1984), p. 47.

icebreaker activity. A variation is paired introductions: Participants are given a few minutes to become acquainted with the person seated next to them, and then each person introduces his or her partner. Some people find this easier than talking about themselves.

Other icebreaker activities include games, short quizzes (followed by open discussion of the answers), or brainstorming sessions ("What are the biggest problems you have with closing sales?"). One management consultant uses a jelly-bean jar as a prop and asks participants to "guess the number of beans in the jar." She relates the number of beans to some figure that is relevant to her particular audience, that is, the company's projected sales volume for the next year. She also presents a prize for the closest guess.

Remember, use icebreaker activities judiciously. Some audiences are full of anticipation and talkative from the beginning; they don't need any warmups. Others may feel it's a waste of time to play games. Whatever you devise, make it more than a "getting to know you" exercise. Use it as an opportunity to learn the participants' expectations and the resources they bring to the workshop.

Once you make it through the first 10 or 20 minutes, the rest of your presentation should be easy. Your problem won't be what to say, but how to fit it all in.

One closing thought about openings. Practice and practice. Know *exactly* what you're going to say from the moment you step up in front of the group—don't leave it to chance. Rehearse your introductory lines over and over until you can say them without stumbling. Then you'll be over the hump. The rest will follow spontaneously.

Chapter Ten

Quitting While You're Ahead

The single worst crime a presenter can commit is to be boring. The second worst is speaking too long.

The human attention span is finite. After a certain length of time, even the most enthralling presentation grows tedious. So don't set out to share everything that's ever been known about your subject. Just hit the high points. Otherwise, you risk the likelihood that people will remember not what you said, but how long you took to say it!

You know that it's time to quit when:

. . . members of the audience begin shifting restlessly in their seats.

. . . three or more persons glance at their wristwatches.

. . . you've said what you came to say (but not, heaven knows, all that you *could* say) on the subject.

. . . the clock shows it's 5 or 10 minutes before the workshop is slated to end

The clock is your best ally. Begin making your summary and closing comments about 10 minutes before the scheduled adjournment. It's better to end 10 minutes early than to run into overtime. If you end early, the audience won't feel short-changed. They'll assume you delivered your message succinctly and efficiently, with time to spare.

On the other hand, ending late shows a disregard for their other commitments. It's as if you're saying, "What we're doing here is more important than anything else you have planned." Audiences are sure to resent this. You worked hard in the past hours to win their favor. Don't blow it in the home stretch.

Plan your closing comments as carefully as your introduction. At the beginning of the workshop, you aimed to make people feel welcome, comfortable, and ready to learn. Now, as you draw to a close, plan to leave them with a clear sense of what has been accomplished.

Don't just dribble off lamely with, "Well, that's about all I have to say. . . . " Make it memorable.

What feelings do you want participants to carry away? At the end of a workshop on electrical wiring, the group should feel knowledgeable. If it is a workshop on writing poetry, you'd like them to feel inspired. In most cases, you'd like the audience to leave with a combination of feelings:

- Motivated, to put the new skills they learned into practice.
- Competent, that they can accomplish these goals.
- Happy that they came (not that the workshop is finally ending).
- Good about themselves and the learning experience.

If time allows, this is a good point to turn the floor over to the participants. Ask them to share the one most useful thing they learned from the program, or what changes they expect to make as a result. This activity is best suited to small groups who have been meeting together for an extended period, and who now feel comfortable sharing their thoughts with one another. If it's a class that has been running for several weeks, you might ask what practices they have already put into effect. These testimonials are helpful to you in evaluating the program and making future modifications.

Food puts your ending on an "up" note, if time and budget permit. A wine and cheese gathering at the end of an all-day workshop gives participants a chance to unwind and continue discussions on an informal basis. Serving fruit and cookies after the closing session, like providing coffee and doughnuts at registration, is a way of saying "thanks for coming." Participants don't expect you to provide refreshments at the end of the program. But they won't hold it against you.

Laughter always makes a good ending. It feels good to both the giver and the receiver. Even if the subject matter is fairly serious, a well-chosen, humorous anecdote or punch line can help drive the point—painlessly—home. I observed this during a workshop on dealing with alcoholism. The speaker, a reformed alcoholic, described all of the weird and imaginative tricks he'd devised for hiding away gin bottles and rationalizing his drinking problem. His stories were funny, but they in no way belittled the seriousness of alcoholism. Indeed, they illustrated the dangers of problem drinking more forcefully than any straightforward lecture on the subject.

But humor is only one of many options. The closing minutes of your workshop can also be the time to:

- Summarize and reemphasize the key points of your presentation.
- Plug the organization that sponsored you and announce any future events that may be of interest to the audience.
- Acknowledge any individuals who assisted with your program.
- Challenge the participants to pursue the topic further on their own (and tell them how).
- Thank them for coming.
- Leave them with something to think about.

Your ending comments may convey almost any combination of appreciation or insight, wit or wisdom. But keep them brief! Nothing is more disheartening than the speaker who wishes to "leave you with one last thought"—and the thought turns into an oration.

The key is to always leave your audience wishing for more, while at the same time feeling as if they've gained more than they expected.

Take a tip from the composers of Broadway musicals, who purposely hold their most rousing, memorable tune for the grand finale. When the patrons leave the theater, they're walking to the beat of that final number. Your goal is the same. Leave them humming!

Chapter Eleven

Evaluations

You can tell. You *know* it went well. You can tell by the looks on the participants' faces that the workshop was a success. They listened attentively; they nodded in agreement. The room was charged with energy. The discussion was focused and substantive.

What further proof do you need that the program went well? You need it in writing.

Visual and verbal feedback can give you a general impression of success or failure. But a written appraisal-form elicits specific recommendations. It not only asks, "Was this okay, or wasn't it?" but "How can I make this better?"

You need to know, whether you're conducting the workshop for the first time or the two hundredth. Many people are tempted to forgo this ritual after they've been teaching awhile. "I've done this so many times, I can tell what works and what doesn't," they insist. But after giving 200 workshops, presenters can sound polished, or they can sound jaded. If they sound jaded, the audience should have an opportunity to tell them so.

Other conclude that as long as no one complains, or gets up and leaves before the program is finished, the workshop was a roaring success. "No news is good news," they convince themselves hopefully. This is a cop-out. Even the best programs have margins for improvement.

Each bit of feedback helps you to hone your program to better fit the participants' needs. Which parts of the presentation were most effective? Would they have preferred more information on certain topics? Did other segments drag a bit? Did you allow for enough group participation? Did you let one or two people monopolize the discussion?

You can't change the workshop to please everyone in attendance. But when you see patterns to their suggestions, modifications may be in order.

SO FAR, SO GOOD

Consciously or subconsciously, you are evaluating the workshop the whole time it's in progress. You listen for comments that indicate approval and agreement. When participants look confused, it signals you to slow down and offer further explanation. If they look bored, you move on to a fresh topic. You can solicit verbal evaluations midway through the workshop, if you wish, by just asking: "Is this addressing the problems most of you came here with? Are there other issues you would like to cover?"

The participants are appraising the program as it goes along also. They are thinking: "Boy, am I glad I came!" or, "When are we going to get to the next subject?" or, "I wonder what we're having for lunch?"

You can't read their minds, so give them an opportunity to transfer these thoughts onto paper. A written evaluation form, to be filled in at the conclusion of the program, is an easy, nonthreatening way for participants to answer your main, all-encompassing question: *How was it?*

DESIGN YOUR OWN QUESTIONNAIRE

An evaluation form should be tailored to your needs and your workshop. Appendix C shows the questionnaire I developed for my time management program. You could use a similar format or modify it as you see fit. Keep in mind the following principals:

Keep it short. Remember, you'll be hitting participants with this questionnaire just as they think they are being dismissed. Some will be eager to offer you their advice and opinions. Others will consider it an imposition. A one-page (and never more than two-page) appraisal sheet won't appear unreasonable.

Include both short-answer and open-ended questions. Some people will make time only to complete short-answer questions—circling multiple-choice responses or checking off yes-or-no replies. Others will be glad to write an essay discussing each part of the program at length, including some issues you never asked about. Create a form that accommodates both kinds of respondents, and leave plenty of space for added comments.

Drafting an evaluation form is a four-step process:

Step one.　　Decide what you need to find out about the effectiveness of your program. For example:

1. Did they enjoy the experience, overall?
2. What were the main things they learned from it?
3. What will they do differently as a result?

Step two.　　Draft questions that will produce the answers you need. Include both short-answer, multiple-choice questions and open-ended questions calling for opinions and suggestions.

Step three.　　Review the questions. Revise or eliminate any that are ambiguous, repetitive, or unnecessary.

Step four.　　Assemble the questionnaire, beginning with general questions and concluding with more specific ones. Keep it simple. Leave plenty of white space. Try to hold the length to one page.

Sample Evaluation Questions

Here in the following are some sample questions that elicit valuable evaluations of your workshop or seminar.

1. How would you rate this program as a whole? (After this question, you could leave a blank space)

Or follow it with a check list:

_____Outstanding

_____Very Good

_____Fair

_____Unsatisfactory

Or follow it with a rating scale:

1	2	3	4	5
unsatisfactory		so-so		excellent

2. Which topics (or parts of the program) did you find most useful?

3. Which topics (or parts of the program) did you find least useful?

Questions 2 and 3 could also be presented as a checklist:

4. How useful did you find the:

	effective	okay	ineffective
Lecture	_____	_____	_____
Group discussion	_____	_____	_____
Small group exercises	_____	_____	_____
Visual aids	_____	_____	_____
Handout materials	_____	_____	_____
(Add your own items)	_____	_____	_____

5. As to group participation, was there:

_____too much

_____not enough

_____a good balance

6. An effective workshop presents theory and practical application. Was there:

_____too much theoretical background

_____too much emphasis on practical application

_____a good balance

7. Were there sufficient opportunities to apply the information presented? Explain:

8. Comment, if you wish, on the instructor:

This type of open-ended question, followed by a blank space, solicits neither praise nor criticism. It may reveal some surprising facts about the way you relate to people.

Alternatively, you could provide a checklist or ask participants to rate the instructor according to a five-point scale, as in question 1.

Question 9 combines closed and open-ended responses, while question 10 calls for specific reactions to elements of your teaching style:

9. Was the instructor effective or ineffective? Explain:

10. Did the instructor seem:

	yes	sometimes	no
knowledgeable in the subject matter	___	___	___
well organized and prepared	___	___	___
interested in alternative viewpoints	___	___	___
helpful and enthusiastic	___	___	___
supportive of the students' progress	___	___	___

11. Did the program meet your needs?

_____yes; very relevant

_____to some extent

_____not at all

12. Were the facilities satisfactory or unsatisfactory? Explain:

13. What improvements would you suggest?

14. How did you learn about this program?

_____brochure

_____friend

_____previous program

_____newspaper ad

_____radio announcement

15. What other program topics would interest you?

16. What persons or organizations might we add to our mailing list?

From these 16 questions you should be able to derive 5 or 10 for a useful evaluation form. Include only the ones which seem applicable to your own needs. Question 14 is relevant only if you are rethinking your marketing techniques. Question 15 is useful if you are planning to revise your subject matter. Remember, the shorter the form, the more willing your participants will be to complete it!

OTHER FORMS OF FEEDBACK

You can measure the effectiveness of your program in other ways besides the written evaluation form. One is to solicit verbal feedback from the participants during and after the program. A second is to review the event on your own after it has ended.

By "soliciting verbal feedback" I mean informally asking the participants questions like, "How's it going? Is this answering some of the questions you came in with? What did you think of the role-playing exercise? Did you enjoy the film?" Often you can ask these questions while the workshop is in process. ("How many of you plan to try this procedure at your office tomorrow?") You can also speak with individual participants at lunch or during one of the breaks. Find an ally within your audience—perhaps the person who arranged your presentation—to help measure the group's reaction to the program, and listen for specific comments.

If you've been hired to give a series of inservice training seminars for an organization and you want to build a strong, ongoing relationship, try setting up some means of speaking with participants after the program is concluded. This could mean gathering a few people for a drink at the end of the workshop, or convening a "focus group"—five or six selected participants—a few days later. These individuals can point out the strengths and weaknesses of the program and share the reactions they have heard from others who attended the program. You can also find out what needs remain unresolved in the organization. These issues may form the base of your next program.

Besides getting valuable guidance and constructive criticism, you're letting participants know that yours is not a static program. You're constantly seeking ways to improve it, and you value their input.

Finally, don't overlook your most immediate source of enlightenment: yourself. You were there. Even though you were busy conducting the workshop, you still had a sense of the audience's reaction: What did they seem to like? What should be changed in the future? So preserve a few quiet minutes in the evening to review the experience.

Ask yourself:

1. Which subjects seemed to hit home and hold participants' attention? At which points did I seem to be losing people?
2. Were there questions I wasn't prepared to answer? Topics that seemed to attract interest that I should bone up on for future programs?
3. How was the pacing? Did I spend too much time on some subjects, causing parts of the workshop to drag and leaving too little time to cover other important issues?

Keep a personal notebook for recording these impressions, or fill out one of your own evaluation forms and tuck it away in a special folder. The notes you make to yourself don't need to be lengthy or soul-searching. Think of them as a tipsheet: things to remember to help future workshops go even more smoothly.

Your personal notebook or folder is also the place to collect anecdotes or comments from participants. If someone in your audience says something that is particularly funny or poignant, that seems to draw a rush of agreement, write it down before you forget it. Incorporate it in your next presentation.

Stress the positive. You'll be reviewing these notes as you prepare for future workshops. That's a point when you'll need encouragement, not a rundown of past mistakes. Every entry of "what went wrong" should be accompanied by "what to try next time."

BRACE YOURSELF

One point remains to be made about evaluations: Some of them are going to be negative. Expect this, and don't allow yourself to feel devastated.

You should anticipate some constructive criticism for three reasons:

1. You're asking for it. If your evaluation form says: "How can I make this program better?"—most people will feel obliged to tell you. You can't expect everyone to reply: "It's perfect just the way it is!"

2. People are different. Within any group, a certain proportion will have different needs, tastes, and reactions to your program. There is no way you can please everybody.

3. Even the best adult learning programs have room for improvement. "Studies have shown that the majority of people will not give anything they are asked to judge the highest rating," trainer Robert L. Burpee says. "If they like something a lot, they are more likely to give it a 9 on a 10-point scale, always leaving a margin for something slightly better."

Here are some more observations from professional trainers on the evaluation process:

Ken Jones: You look straight past the twelve appraisal forms that give the workshop a high "5" rating and stare at the one that's marked "3." Instead of being pleased by the high success ratio, you think, "How did I fail that person? What did I do wrong?"

Tess Kirby: I always throw out the best and throw out the worst and focus on the ones in the middle. I advise new trainers in our department to do the same. Once I forgot to warn a new staff person that she should *expect* some criticism. She was in a funk for days over a negative comment.

Fred Steingold: You have to expect that the personal traits that appeal to some members of the audience will be the same ones that put other people off. One evaluation form will say "I like his serious manner." "Too dry," declares another.

Bob Burpee: I hate evaluations. They're like reviews of plays. They nitpick, giving more attention to the minor flaws than the overall content. Naturally, you want people to leap to their feet and applaud, exclaiming, "This is the most brilliant thing I have ever experienced!" Remember that a low rating may have nothing to do with you. It could be a reflection of the mood the person was in. Maybe he had a fight with his kids that morning. Maybe you remind him of his Aunt Marge, and he hates Aunt Marge. You'll never win him over.

Fran Scherger adds that you should "ask for criticism, but also find out what you did right. Collect testimonials." Scherger includes the following request on her evaluation sheets:

> Please write the most wonderful thing you can (in all good conscience) say about this seminar:
>
> _____
>
> _____
>
> _____
>
> Can we use your name? If yes, sign: Name: _____
>
> Title:_____
>
> Organization:_____

Signed testimonials provide good copy for brochures and other promotional materials, Scherger points out.

> _Marla Rubenstein:_ It's a personal risk to hand out those evaluation forms. It's very threatening, putting yourself on the line. But without some criticism, you never will grow. Anyone can benefit from being told, "Here's what you're doing right. Here's how to make it better."

Many people plug away at a job for years and never hear if their work is good, bad, or indifferent. Others receive an annual performance review. Training and development is one of the very few fields that provide a mechanism for continuous feedback. Welcome it. It's all part of the learning experience.

Chapter Twelve

Bombs Away!

You have to take chances to succeed in any business. Yet compared to gunrunning or sky diving, seminars do not seem so risky. What's the worst thing that could happen to you? What could possibly go wrong?

> You wake up the morning of the workshop with severe laryngitis.
>
> Your car breaks down on the freeway as you are driving to the seminar site.
>
> You arrive 30 minutes after the program was scheduled to begin.
>
> The microphone makes a shrill whine like an air-raid siren.
>
> The slide projector seems to be giving off smoke instead of light.
>
> Eyeing the clock, you notice you are running behind schedule. You'll never be able to cover all the material on the agenda.
>
> Or worse: You're about to make your closing comments and you realize you have 30 more minutes to fill!

Everyone who has ever been involved in giving workshops has horror stories to tell. "Horror" doesn't seem an overstatement. Little things like a dead microphone achieve crisis status when you're in the spotlight and a roomful of strangers is observing your discomfort. This chapter is intended to forewarn you of the typical things that can go wrong during a presentation, so that you can:

1. Anticipate them.
2. Prevent them whenever possible.
3. Keep your sense of humor when they happen anyway.

There's no substitute for experience, except perhaps someone else's experience.

GOING FOR BROKE

Like the other persons profiled in this book, Margaret Tyler is real. Her name has been changed since she would just as soon forget this experience. Any similarity to any other unlucky person named Tyler is a coincidence.

Tyler was 30, single, and had spent several years in teaching and public relations when she decided to go into the workshop business. The focus of her program was "career transitions." She planned a series of all-day seminars priced at $50 per enrollee that would feature practical information on job hunting, resume writing, and interviewing skills. The year was 1982, most of the country was in a recession, and thousands of people were laid off from their jobs. Tyler saw everyone drawing an unemployment check as a potential workshop participant.

Her ideas seemed sound. To her friends, her staff, and other associates, she seemed to be doing everything right. She laid groundwork carefully, gaining support from several state agencies and professional associations who promised to help publicize her program. She took out a loan to cover the costs of an impressive-looking office, brochures, mailing lists, and an answering service.

She wanted to go first class. "I want people to come away feeling good about themselves, with a fresh, positive outlook," she insisted. You can't motivate people to feel optimistic in a dreary borrowed auditorium, she reasoned, so she reserved a room in the city's top hotel and ordered a banquet-style lunch for the hundred or more participants she expected. Then, propelled by her own enthusiasm, she scheduled four seminars in four cities during July and August, mailed out 8000 brochures, and waited for the checks to roll in.

And waited.

The registration deadline came and with less than a week before the first seminar, she counted three paid participants. She faced two choices:

1. Cancel, return the $150 in paid fees, and take a big loss.
2. Hold the seminar for three people.

Some last-minute inquiries caused her to forge ahead. As the day of the seminar drew near, Tyler began getting phone calls from people who claimed they were anxious—in fact, desperate—to attend. Elated, Tyler told them they could register the day of the conference. These verbal assurances raised the potential enrollment to at least 20, she figured. She decided to guarantee an attendance of 30 at the hotel.

Three people showed up. Six, counting Tyler and her two staff members.

What went wrong? Tyler had researched the need, advertised as widely as she knew how, and assembled a credible, substantive program. In retrospect, she has identified some of her mistakes:

Price. People who are unemployed may be hesitant to pay $50 to attend a workshop—even one aimed at helping them find a job.

Timing. July and August are probably the worst months (next to December) for scheduling a workshop. Many people are on vacation. Those who aren't are thinking more about recreational pursuits, not attending educational programs.

Marketing. Direct mail is rarely an effective way to promote a seminar unless the mailing list is precisely targeted. Tyler mailed her brochure to a cross-section of addresses within certain Zip code areas. She may as well have scattered them from an airplane. A workshop on a general topic such as career transitions is better publicized by a newspaper ad or a press release.

Blind optimism. Tyler should have test-marketed her workshop on a smaller scale rather than investing so much money and effort into a lavish production. Had she tried one small local program rather than aiming for statewide attendance, her loss would have been small, in proportion to her investment.

One of Tyler's biggest and costliest mistakes was relying on verbal assurances. It's okay to accept registrations at the door, but don't count on them as a means of meeting expenses. When people don't pay in advance, they are very likely to back out at the last minute.

HOW TO BE BORING—A TRAINER'S TIPSHEET

I led off with Tyler's experience because it was a full-scale stunning flop. It makes every other catastrophe we will mention in this chapter seem trivial by comparison. I hope it will make your own mistakes seem trivial as well. It's psychologically healthy to look at them in this context, even if, at the time they occur, they seem devastating.

"The worst workshop I ever presented," says John Reed, a Seattle-based consultant, "was on collective decision-making. It was only my fourth or fifth presentation; I was young and still pretty nervous. It was also the first program I had conducted on this subject," he relates, "so while I had studied up on it, I sure didn't consider myself an expert. I was very uneasy about being asked questions I couldn't answer.

"So I decided not to give anyone an opportunity to ask questions," Reed recalls. "I just talked, nonstop, for two hours!"

Two hours?! "Yep. That was my other mistake! I thought this way I'd be giving them their money's worth. I just barreled along without taking a break. No wonder they spent the last hour of the workshop shifting in their seats and looking desperate!"

He remembers other details of that incident. The audience was a group of 30 high school teachers who were required to attend by the school's vice-principal. Reed heard many of them muttering when they arrived about papers that needed grading and other "more important things to do." They were openly indifferent to the subject matter and resentful about being told to attend.

Moreover, the workshop was scheduled from 1 to 3 P.M.—a slump period of the day when many people find it hard to be alert and attentive for anything. The facilities weren't very conducive to learning either. The workshop was held in the school cafeteria.

Later that evening, Reed reviewed his experience and made a list of "things to do differently in the future." It included:

1. Never stick with straight lecturing. It's deadly boring for the participants, exhausting for me.

2. Get participants at each table to raise issues about group decision-making that they have experienced at school, with their own administration. This will make the discussion that follows seem more relevant.

3. Don't be afraid of questions I can't answer. I have two options:
    a. Admit I don't have the answers; promise to find out the information and get back to them.
    b. Toss it back to the audience. Maybe someone else has a good response.

4. Never, ever go two hours without taking a break.

5. When I sense some hostility or apathy in an audience, I should acknowledge it and try to direct the subject matter to issues that interest them more instead of pretending not to notice. It may not change their attitude, but it might establish a better rapport.

"Rapport" is a nebulous yet highly important connecting link between you and your audience. It puts you "on the same wavelength" with them. Sometimes it is established easily and immediately through your appearance, your demeanor, your opening lines. Sometimes it's more difficult.

"Some groups are much tougher than others," Kenneth W. Jones states. "When the audience is much older than you are, or perceives themselves to be of a different status, you may have to work very hard to establish credibility."

Jones, a professional in the field of training and development, had recently conducted a preretirement seminar for a group of university professors. From the start, he could sense their aloofness. Who was he, a young man in his early thirties, to advise *them* about planning their future? Jones's seminars on other topics were always highly rated, but with this group, he struck out. The evaluations were among the lowest he'd ever received. About this experience, Jones observes:

> When you know that your program has failed, you go through a series of feelings.
>
> Despair. Why am I even bothering with this kind of work?
>
> Resentment. Why didn't they tell me I was on the wrong track? If they weren't interested in the subject, why didn't they say so? Why didn't they ask more questions?
>
> Determination. Next time it will be different. Next time I will send out questionnaires in advance to participants and ask them what specific problems they would like to see addressed. Then I'll be certain to cover those issues.

The message: Don't overlook your mistakes, but don't dwell on them either. Allow yourself a short period of intense regret (five minutes should do it) and then pack them away. Treat each of your failures as a valuable learning experience.

AN OUNCE OF PREVENTION...

Many full-blown disasters can be traced to tiny errors in judgment. If I could offer one piece of all-purpose advice to help ward off problems, it's this: Be early. Figure out exactly how much time you need to pack your materials, to review your lines, and to get where you're going. Then give yourself an extra 30 minutes.

Once—just once—I failed to calculate the exact mileage between my home and a seminar site. I glanced at the map and figured the distance at 30 miles. It may have been 30 miles as the crow flies, but it turned out to be over 50 miles as the car travels, on winding two-lane country roads. Darkness fell as I wended my way that evening, and so did the rain, forcing me to downshift to 30 miles per hour.

Two more oversights: When I finally reached the city, I had to find the community college where I was to speak. And once I reached the college, I had to find the classroom.

I arrived, wet and exhausted, 20 minutes after the workshop was scheduled to begin. Astonishingly, the group was still patiently waiting. They were warm and sympathetic; everyone can relate to the distress of being late and lost. But in my mind, my credibility was shot. You do not arrive 20 minutes late to teach a workshop on time management!

Based on my own trials and errors and those related by others in the seminar business, here is a checklist to help you prevent some of the most common—and avoidable—mistakes. It's far from all-inclusive. Add your own notes at the end.

How to Avert a Catastrophe
(or Even a Minor Crisis)

1. Don't arrive late. (Late is anything less than 20 minutes early.)

2. Don't start late. I once attended a conference that was scheduled to begin at 9 A.M. At 9:15, the organizer of the event stepped up to the microphone and announced, "We're going to wait about 10 or 15 more minutes because we're expecting a few more participants." Well. Those of us who were already assembled exchanged glances, and it was clear we were all thinking the same thing. We were on time! Why were we being penalized and the latecomers rewarded?

3. Don't run into overtime. Failure to begin or end on time shows a lack of respect for the participants and for the fact that they may have other commitments. Naturally, they will resent this.

4. Don't make people regroup once they are comfortably seated. You can tell by the friendly patter that the participants are sitting with people they know. You think they should use this occasion to make new acquaintances. You're right, but remember, the real purpose of this event is learning. You are the

teacher, not a shipboard social director. Most adults feel they are too old to play musical chairs.

5. Don't try to cover too many subjects within too short a time frame. People should leave feeling knowledgeable, not overwhelmed.

6. If you are traveling by air to give your presentation in another city, bring all your essential equipment with you as carry-on luggage. This includes notes, slides or overheads, and at least one set of handouts. If the rest of your handouts are lost or delayed in transit, you can at least have new copies made after your arrival.

7. Don't leave your equipment to chance. If it's being provided by the hotel or conference center, arrive early enough to make sure it's there and it's what you expected. If you're using electronic gear, practice ahead of time so that you know exactly how it operates. How can you come across as an authority if you can't thread the film projector?

8. If you're using a screen or a video monitor, be sure you know where the light switches are.

9. Invest in your own equipment, if you plan to make lots of presentations that rely on visual aids. The cost is justified by the peace of mind that comes from knowing the easel is the right size for your flipchart, the slide projector is loaded and ready to go.

10. In the course of your presentation, do involve participants as much as possible.

11. Don't belittle or reject anything they have to say.

12. Don't be sarcastic.

13. Don't use sexist language or connotation. Be careful about referring to a boss as "he." Don't use "girls" when you mean "women." Avoid the distinction "working and nonworking women," which implies housekeeping is not work. Substitute the words "unemployed" or "women who don't work outside the home."

14. Never make a joke that can be even remotely interpreted as an ethnic, racial, or sexual slur.

Chapter Thirteen

Dealing with Problem Participants

"Pssst. Bzzz bzzzzzzzzzzz pst. Bzzzzzzzzzzz . . ."

That's how it sounded from where I stood. I was in the front of the classroom teaching strategies of decision making and scribbling notes on the blackboard while a low hum of conversation emanated from one of the back rows. A woman with blonde frizzy hair was engaged in a dialogue with her companion in the next seat—not loud enough for me to distinguish the words, but loud enough to be audible and distracting.

What were they talking about? Were they saying that this was the best program they had ever attended? Or that my conclusions were completely erroneous? Maybe they were discussing a movie they'd seen last weekend. I couldn't tell, and that made the persistent hum even more disconcerting.

Side conversations are one of several kinds of vexing behaviors you're likely to encounter in the course of presenting workshops. This chapter will suggest some ways to deal with them, along with other types of problem participants. These include:

The monopolizer.   This person almost always answers first, talks too often and too long, leaving the rest of the class little chance to say anything.

The extremely shy, quiet participant.   The mirror opposite of the monopolizer is so uncommunicative that you're hard pressed to tell if he or she is getting anything at all out of the workshop.

The rambler.   Give ramblers the floor, and they drift off on a tangent.

The arguer. Not really quarrelsome, this person wants to explore both sides of every issue. But like the rambler, he or she can often steer the discussion into irrelevant side topics.

The antagonist. People who are antagonists do not merely disagree with you, like arguers; they don't like you. They don't even want to be in the workshop and resent you for wasting their time.

Each of these people and situations poses a challenge. (Think of them that way—as a challenge, not a crisis.) You can't screen your audience in advance, in most cases, so there's no telling when any of these individuals will pop up in your workshop. When they do, they will still take you by surprise.

Does it help to anticipate problem participants and have a preplanned counteroffensive? Or do you wait until the situation confronts you and hope you can think on your feet?

I say, forewarned is forearmed. The next few pages will describe the types of rude or hostile behavior you *may* encounter and suggest ways of diffusing it without losing your cool. You may not be able to avoid it, but you'll recall what steps to take after it happens.

SIDE CONVERSATIONS

The episode that began this chapter is true, and at the time it occurred I had no idea how to handle it. I was very new to the business of presenting workshops and far from overconfident. I tried to ignore the buzz of conversation in the rear of the room, but whenever I glanced toward the whispering parties, I lost my train of thought. Finally I blurted, "I'm sorry, but it's difficult for me to explain this material while the two of you are talking! It's very distracting." The two looked startled, embarrassed, and then fell blessedly silent.

Sometimes, the direct approach is the most effective.

Often, the rest of the audience will rally to your support. (They were wondering how long it would take you to say something.) They will reinforce your message with their own reactions: "Yes! Keep it down back there. It's difficult to hear!" Sometimes they will shush the offending parties before you are forced to say anything.

The tone you set at the beginning of the workshop will cue people on how to conduct themselves. If you allow a steady stream of chatter to go on as you are introducing the subject, the audience will presume talking during the presentation is acceptable. If you pause and wait in silence for the conversation to die down, they'll get the message. If it's a particularly rowdy group, be as aggressive as they are. Say cheerfully, "Hey! I have a lot of important things to share with you, but I can't get started until I have everybody's attention!"

The seating arrangements in your room will either encourage or deter side conversations. As Chapter Eight points out, people feel more comfortable about talking when they are seated in circular arrangements. If the room is set up with several round tables, the participants will probably sit with people they know and will feel more inclined to contribute to the group discussions.

But they will also feel freer to make comments to those seated nearby, even as you are talking. How do you discourage this? Dean Osterman, who conducts workshops on "Discussion Management," advises, "Stand by the talkative table. People aren't likely to continue a conversation when you're standing at their elbow."

Osterman feels that moving among the tables as he speaks creates a rapport with the audience. It dissolves the artificial barriers that often seem to exist when a presenter remains rigidly at one end of the room and the group is confined to the other. But it also deters side conversations because, since he's mobile, he's unpredictable. People pay attention as he speaks because, as he points out, "they never know where I'm going to pop up next!"

It may help to consider *why* side conversations occur. Maybe the members of the group are bored. (Are you boring?) Or tired. (Is it time to take a break?) Maybe they have something to say, but you've been barreling ahead nonstop and they haven't had a chance. Create an atmosphere that encourages participants to raise their hands and express their ideas openly instead of whispering to one another.

If a side conversation lasts only a minute, it's best to ignore it. But if it persists and begins to cause a disturbance, you can pause and say, "I'm sorry. I couldn't hear what you said. How about sharing it with the rest of us?"

The talker may repeat his comments before the whole group, or he may decline. In either case, you're not scolding him; you're simply reinforcing the rules of the meeting—that is, "If you've got something to say, say it to everyone!"

MONOPOLIZERS, RAMBLERS, AND ARGUERS

There are two kinds of monopolizers: those who know a lot about your subject and those who *think* they know a lot about it. For both types, your class provides a forum and a captive audience.

You can usually spot monopolizers early on from their eager-beaver attitude. They leap in at every pause to insert an opinion or supply an answer—sometimes before you've even asked the question. Or they may politely raise their hands and gain permission to speak . . . and not stop. Their comments grow and swell into a speech . . . an inaugural address.

In a subtle way, monopolizers are vying with you for leadership of the group. ("I'm the *real* expert here," each implies.) If you capitulate, you lose credibility with the rest of the class. They came to hear you, and expect you to stay in control. If you don't, none of *them* will get a chance to take part in the discussion.

Ramblers monopolize a discussion also, but they add their own special note of confusion to the proceedings. Their reasoning is not always clear; the point they are making, ambiguous. They digress onto some tangential or personal matter that is of no interest to the rest of the group.

Finally, there's the arguer. You probably know at least one person who falls in this category: contentious Uncle Harry, who just loves a debate. If you say the weather's hot, Harry will insist it's chilly, just to be obstinate. Sometimes he truly disagrees with you. Often he's just playing devil's advocate.

Arguers may bring some depth to a discussion, causing the group to consider new sides to an issue. But often they are just nitpickers, diverting attention away from more important subjects. Arguers chip away at your authority by putting you continuously on the defensive.

Any of these individuals threaten your authority in fact, because, if you allow them to hoard the spotlight, you risk alienating everyone else in attendance. You may have to be as strong-willed as they are in order to keep the discussion on course. Don't let a persistent, highly vocal minority divert you from the interests of the group as a whole. Here are some strategies to use:

With the nonstop talker: Chime in, finish his thought, and quickly say something affirming like, "I agree with you there." Then follow with an observation of your own or say, "Anyone like to add to that?" Like a player on the basketball court, your objective is to steal the conversational ball away during a fast dribble and toss it to someone else on the team. Interrupting is not the most polite means of managing a discussion, but with the monopolizer, it's often the only tactic that works.

If the monopolizer or the rambler pauses long enough for you to get a word in, ask her to summarize. "So what would you say is your main point?"

Or summarize it yourself. "Let me see if I understand you, Joyce. You would prefer . . ." Then restate her comments briefly in your own words, and ask Joyce if she agrees with your synopsis. If she does, throw the issue before the group and get their reactions—or move on to a new topic.

Sometimes a discussion gets sidetracked because one member of the group misunderstands a point or has a personal problem to solve. Don't let yourself get pulled into a personal discussion with one individual at the expense of everyone else. Let the group decide: "Should we pursue this line of discussion or move on with the agenda, and Mary and I can talk about it later during lunch?" It could be that the group is interested in Mary's problem and is curious about how you'd handle it. If that's the case, talk about it now. Otherwise, speak with her privately later. Either way, Mary's needs are addressed and the full group's interests are served.

Finally, when dealing with any type of overzealous talker, don't rule out the direct approach. "I appreciate all your comments, Carl, but I'd like to hear from some of the others. Who else has something to add?"

THE SILENT TREATMENT

Overtalkative participants can be troublesome, but at least you know where they stand. You don't have to second guess whether they are following the material or agree with you. They tell you—often much more than you wanted to know.

Silent members of the group can be more disconcerting. You can't tell *what* they're thinking.

Some workshop participants may be quiet because:

- They are shy and unassertive by nature.
- They aren't interested in the subject.
- They are thinking about other things.
- They don't understand what you're talking about.
- They understand, but they are slow at collecting their thoughts and expressing them verbally. By the time they decide what to say, someone else has said it.

As a group leader, you must try to sense whether an individual is quiet by choice—some people prefer to be observers rather than active participants in the group process—or whether they want to speak up but never get an opportunity.

When you're working with a large group and a tight schedule, it's impractical and unnecessary to rope everyone into the discussion. But if it's a class that is meeting over a period of several weeks, and you're trying to instill a feeling of unity and common purpose, you'll want to take measures to make sure even the quieter members of the group feel involved.

Set the tone at the beginning of the first class. Let participants know that you welcome and expect sharing of ideas. Clarify the objectives of the session and create a friendly, non-threatening atmosphere. Going around the room with group introductions or a question that each person answers in turn is a good icebreaker. Dividing up into small groups of three or four also gives the quiet person a chance to speak up in a less intimidating arena. By directing a yes-or-no question at the quiet member occasionally, you solicit his opinions without pressuring him to contribute a lengthy comment.

Sometimes you'll be faced with a room full of stoney, silent people. Don't panic or despair. Try to figure out the reason. Are they quiet because they are tired? Bored? Disinterested? You can usually tell from their facial expressions. Fatigue has a glazed look about it. Disinterest wears a frown of apathy, even resentment.

You'll have to work harder to win over a silent group. Sometimes you can tease them out of their stupor: "The question I'm most often asked by groups like this is ...? How many of you would agree with that? Come on, I should see some heads nodding!"

Be patient with these people. They may be remaining quiet because they don't know one another well and they're unfamiliar with the subject. Rather than reveal their ignorance, they want to hear what *you* have to say.

After all, that's the reason they came.

THE FRONTAL ASSAULT

As you prepare for a workshop, naturally, you hope the audience will like you and learn from you. At worst, you figure some people may be indifferent. You certainly don't expect anyone to be hostile.

Yet sometimes, the signs of hostility are unmistakable: arms folded across the chest; the skeptical frown; cold silence. What have you done to deserve this?

Participant hostility is probably not directed at you personally, but at the workshop topic. You have been contracted to conduct a learning experience. Certain members of the audience feel they know enough about the subject already or that they don't need to know about it in the first place. You're an imposition, a waste of their time.

When you sense these feelings, acknowledge them. "I can see some of you don't feel this applies to your situation. Since we're here to solve problems, what are some of your other concerns?" Show them that you're flexible, and you may be able to turn their hostility around and gain their support.

Involve everyone in the process. Divide the participants into small groups and have each group define the problems it wants to see addressed. Write these objectives on newsprint and tape them to the front wall. Then, let the full group vote on which objectives have the highest priority, and construct a new agenda. People tend to be more supportive of an educational program if they helped create it.

Another tip: Enlist some of the more recalcitrant participants as group leaders or assign them some other role in the proceedings. It's the old philosophy: If you can't lick 'em, join 'em. But you're getting them to join you!

It also helps to share a little about your own background, expectations, and goals. It's much easier for the group to resent an outsider and an aloof authority figure. If you reveal yourself as a real human being, they're apt to decide they like you. Then the program can move forward in an atmosphere of mutual respect.

Sometimes, of course, there are holdouts. Sometimes you will be confronted by an individual who remains stubbornly resistant, antagonistic to the end. This person seems bent on embarrassing you and sabotaging the program.

Reasoning probably won't help. You'll just find yourself on the defensive, carrying on a private argument in front of the whole group. It's better to defer the entire issue until later: "It looks like we hold different points of view. Why don't we discuss it over lunch?"

Colleen Stafford found herself faced off against a hostile participant in a workshop she was conducting on "Community Leadership Development." It was hardly a meeting that would have been expected to spark controversy, so the sudden outburst from a woman in the rear row caught Stafford completely off guard. Here's her account.

The Saboteur

"The whole purpose of the community leadership workshop was to develop a sense of group unity and commitment to a series of programs. The expectation was that future sessions would build on what they had accomplished during that first meeting," Stafford explains. The morning had gone well, and she was on the brink of that good, satisfied feeling you get when you work hard and have accomplished what you intended.

Without warning, a woman in the back of the room slowly rose from her chair. Drawing herself up to her full height of about six feet, she boomed out imperiously, "This has been a complete waste of time!"

Stafford was speechless. The interruption was destructive of everything she had been working to create. Even worse, the woman went on to insult the rest of the participants by saying that the meeting hadn't in any way met her needs and she couldn't understand why *anyone* would benefit.

In retrospect, Stafford hit upon the perfect response. "I should have said, 'My goodness! You must be in the wrong workshop!'"

As it happened, the group came to her rescue. They pulled out copies of the brochure and pointed out that everything on the agenda had been covered. "They were outraged that anyone would challenge their carefully nurtured identity as a group, and wouldn't let her continue," she relates. Recovering her composure somewhat, Stafford resumed her wrapup and set objectives for future sessions.

Stafford's experience points up the following realities about problem participants that bear repeating:

- You can't anticipate them. Like a rear-end collision, they'll happen to you when least expected.
- You can't avoid them.
- You can't change them—certainly not in a short-term workshop.
- You can't allow them to steal all your attention at the expense of the rest of the participants.
- You *can* divert them, cool their tempers, and try to channel their energy toward your objectives.
- You can survive them.

Chapter Fourteen

Conquering Stage Fright

Your heart pounds, your palms sweat, your throat feels dry and raspy. You feel as though there is a tennis match going on inside your stomach. Any minute now, your knees will give way and you'll pass out, unconscious.

Is this the onset of some exotic new illness? No, it's something many people find far more dreadful: speaking in public.

It seems to be a well-documented, almost universal phobia. "When a market research team asked 3,000 Americans what they feared most, 41 percent named 'speaking before a group,'" reports communications consultant Jeanne L. McClaran. "It ranked first and worst—ahead of heights, financial problems, insects, deep water, sickness, death and flying!"

So if you feel a little nervous about making your presentation—welcome to the club!

First the bad news: You may never completely get over it. That's the consensus of everyone I've surveyed, including three people who conduct workshops on public speaking.

"I think you're in trouble if you reach the point that you don't feel nervous," McClaran says. "It gets the adrenaline flowing and can lead to a more lively, thoughtful presentation. That sense of anticipation is evidence that you care about your subject and your audience."

And that's the good news. You can make this nervous energy work for you, not against you. You can bring it under control.

Dorothy Sarnoff, the nationally known speech and image

consultant who has coached show business personalities, prime ministers, and presidents, states:

> There are two kinds of nervousness. Positive nervousness, racehorse nervousness, an almost trembling eagerness to be off and running—that's productive. The adrenaline flows, the brain is acute, the reflexes quick, the eyes bright. That kind of intense excitement adds luster to your presentation.
>
> Negative nervousness paralyzes. It's the knot in the pit of your stomach, the sinking feeling. It makes your palms sweat, your throat and lips dry. It freezes your face, gives your eyes a look of panic, maks your heart feel as though it will burst. Negative nervousness dulls the responses and perceptions, numbs the judgment, turns the body into an awkward, inept betrayer. It creates the overwhelming urge to run away.
>
> It's a protector when you're crossing a street and see a truck coming at you; it's a killer when you face a room full of people. Negative nervousness robs you of authority, effectiveness and poise when you need them most.[1]

Negative nervousness comes from feeling unprepared; from being afraid you'll flub your lines and look foolish and incompetent. The previous chapters aimed at getting you through the preparation phase. At this point, you should know your subject as well as your own life history. You're a walking encyclopedia of hard data, opinions, advice, provocative questions, and practical knowledge.

All you need now is the nerve.

KNOW YOUR AUDIENCE

Preparation means not only knowing what you bring to the audience (i.e., your subject matter) but what to expect from them. Find out all you can about those you will address.

Ask the person who booked your presentation about the makeup of the group. Are they mostly men, women, or both? What is the general age range? How many will be attending?

Are they mostly members of a single profession? Homemakers? Retired persons? College students?

What is the context of the activity you've agreed to take part in? Is it an educational meeting? A social gathering?

One way to gauge the group's expectations is to ask about prior program topics. Do they tend to be humorous? Inspira-

---

[1]Dorothy Sarnoff, *Making the Most of Your Best* (New York: Doubleday, 1981), pp. 75–76.

tional? Serious? Did the previous speaker talk about wine tasting or child abuse? It's useful to know what kind of act you are following.

Likewise, if your presentation is part of an all-day conference, find out what kinds of people are attending and what other programs are on the agenda. At the Educational Association meeting: Will the participants be mostly administrators ... or teachers? It might make a difference in the slant of your presentation. Try to attend the keynote address. It will usually set the tone for the day and may raise issues you can follow up on later, whether you are addressing a plenary session or one of several concurrent workshops.

What if this is a course or workshop you are mounting independently? When you mail out registration forms, include a space for enrollees to indicate something relevant about themselves. If it's a business-related class, this might be the company they represent or the position they hold. For a craft class, you might want to know if they are "beginner" or "advanced." Leave space on the form for "reason for attending," or include a list of topics on which they can circle their main interests. You could call participants personally to confirm their enrollment and, at the same time, find out what they hope to gain from the course. Then you won't feel as if you're facing a room full of strangers on the day of the program.

Many professional speakers and trainers use the time before the program starts to establish a rapport. They greet people at the door. They meet every participant personally, shake hands, memorize names and faces. They give each participant the feeling they are genuinely welcome, an asset to the group. Try it yourself. It creates a warm, friendly atmosphere, a sense of camaraderie between you and the participants. And that will take the edge off your nervousness.

The more you know about your audience, the more at ease you feel. They become not a room full of hostile strangers, but people with whom you share common interests. By focusing your attention on *their* needs, you can forget about your own insecurities. Most of your fears stem from fear of the unknown. Once you know what to expect, you stop worrying about it.

JUST BE YOURSELF

I once attended a conference for which the keynote speaker was a laid-off factory worker. He had never before addressed an audience, yet he had been invited on this occasion because his experience was central to the theme of the conference, "Coping with Unemployment." During the welcoming remarks and introductions he sat on stage, shifting anxiously in his chair. One could tell he was having second thoughts about agreeing to this task. Finally he strode up to the microphone, hesitated, and took a deep breath. Then he blurted, "I guess y'all can tell I'm just nervous as hell about speaking to you folks!"

The audience burst into laughter and he grinned gratefully. From that moment, he had them in the palm of his hand.

Just about everyone recognizes the feeling of stage fright. Admit to it, and most audiences will respond with reassurance and supportiveness.

A colleague of mine related a similar experience—but her story had a postscript.

Carol Collins, 38, is a clinical psychologist in private practice. She achieved local prominence when she was asked to write a newspaper column with advice on family relationships. No sooner did her name start appearing in print, but she began getting requests to address civic groups and conduct workshops. "The first time I agreed, I felt like such an amateur and a nobody. So I thought, 'why put up any pretenses?'" Collins said. "I opened my remarks by stating, 'I'm not talking to you today as a psychotherapist, but as another working parent. I'm not good at making speeches. The only formal address I have given was at my daughter's Brownie Scout Flyup.'"

It worked. The gee-whiz-I'm-nobody-special line—Collins called it her "toe in the sand routine"—brought warmth and sympathy from the audience.

She used it successfully—the same line—at the beginning of five more talks that year. Then she was asked to address a Kiwanis dinner for 200 people. That evening, her self-effacing opening line seemed to fall flat. She recalls, "I apologized for my neophyte status and instead of responding with sympathetic laughter, the audience looked embarrassed for me. The line didn't ring true any more. I wasn't an amateur any longer, and they didn't want me to be. They came to hear an expert!"

The moral: You can use your nervousness to connect with the audience. But don't try to fool them with it. The last time Collins tried to pass herself off as a "shy beginner," nobody bought it. Her credibility was hurt instead of enhanced.

Since then she has begun to accept herself for what she is: an authority in her field.

OFF TO A SHAKY START

The physical manifestations of stage fright can be pretty disconcerting. How can you appear cool and confident when your hands are visibly trembling? When your heart is pounding so loudly that you're certain it will drown out anything you have to say? These physical symptoms can be so disorienting that they cause you to lose your composure. The more you worry about appearing nervous, the more nervous you become.

How do you break this cycle?

Here are some methods that work for me. They are not what three out of four doctors recommend, but then, they aren't backed by scientific research. Mostly, they just reflect common sense.

Seven Ways To Reduce Public-speaking Panic

1. If you're nervous, don't mention it. It worked for Joe, the laid-off factory worker, and it worked for Carol at first. But it's not what the audience came to hear. If you don't call attention to your nervousness, they probably won't notice it.

2. Concentrate on appearing calm. Sit erect. Don't fidget with your jewelry or shuffle your note cards. Notice interesting things about the room you're in, the clothes people are wearing. By diverting your attention to your physical surroundings, you take your mind off yourself.

3. Be cautious about what goes into your body. Eat lightly. (Most people have little appetite before speaking, so this is rarely a problem.) Limit yourself to one drink. Alcohol may seem to relax you an hour before your presentation, but it can make you feel sluggish midway through. Too much coffee will increase the jitters—especially on an empty stomach!

4. Don't take tranquilizers, or any kind of medication that promises to "calm your nerves." It could be unsafe or habit-forming. You will certainly never gain self-confidence by becoming drug dependent.

5. Physical exercise is a much better way to reduce stress. Fifteen minutes or more of aerobics—jogging, swimming, even running in place—will help blow off some of that nervous energy. Rotate your shoulders and neck to reduce muscle tension. S-t-r-e-t-c-h your body; then bend from the waist and go limp. (Do not, of course, do these exercises at the podium.)

6. Just before you go on, take a deep breath from the lower part of your chest. Inhale slowly, taking little sips of air. Exhale for as long as you can, as if you are draining every bit of air out of your body. Repeat.

7. If your anxiety was charted on a graph, you would probably notice that it peaks at the beginning of your presentation (or possibly prior to that—as you are being introduced). So if you feel your pulse racing or hear your voice quiver at first, don't panic. Tell yourself—hang in there. It will pass. (And it will!)

UP WITH CONFIDENCE

Physical tension reducers aren't enough. You need a mental exercise program as well. Think of it as a series of mental pushups to shape up your confidence.

You have probably been wearing yourself down with negative messages. "What if I'm not good enough?" "They are probably expecting someone who's lots more polished and articulate." "They will probably be disappointed."

What brings on this self-defeating behavior? It's likely to be force of habit. When you look in the mirror, do you ever notice your straight teeth and winning smile? No. It's the fat thighs, every time.

There may be a time and a place to be self-deprecating. This isn't it.

Put your doubts aside for this occasion. You've worked hard to organize and prepare your material. Now it's time to project yourself with equal conviction—as an authoritative, likeable person. Dorothy Sarnoff says:

> You can project joy, friendliness and empathy by concentrating on four phrases that give out positive vibes. The first two phrases, "I'm glad I'm here. I'm glad you're here," communicate joy and ease. The third, "I care about you," projects concern. The fourth, "I know that I know," gives the message of authority.
>
> Picture these four phrases as spokes of a wheel. Put the wheel like a record on the turntable of your mind, and play it as you repeat the phrases nonstop, over and over. Make yourself feel what you're saying.[2]

Commit these phrases to memory, Sarnoff advises. Say them over and over again like a chant. Synchronize them with your breath-

---

[2]Ibid., pp. 78–79.

ing exercises. Fill your mind with reassurance, leaving no space for the misgivings to return.

Positive self-talk can convert your doubts into a sense of anticipation. But don't just take my word for it:

Spencer Johnson, M.D., co-author of the best-seller *The One Minute Manager,* relates that he still experiences some uneasiness when speaking before groups. But his attitude changed after witnessing an interview with opera singer Beverly Sills. She was in the midst of a demanding tour schedule, appearing in nightly as well as matinee performances.

"Aren't there times when you find yourself wishing you didn't have to sing tonight?" a reporter asked her.

"Not at all," the famous opera singer replied. "I don't say to myself, 'I *have* to sing tonight.' I *get* to sing tonight. I think about what a privilege it is to know that all of these people have come to see me. I feel very appreciative."

From that moment, Johnson relates, he adopted a different mind set. He decided: "I don't have to speak. I get to speak. I began to envision, step by step, members of the audience deciding to come, getting ready, driving to the meeting place. I create a sense of positive anticipation, matching their own."

You see? It's all in your mind. The next time anxieties threaten to creep back into your consciousness, ward them off with positive self-imaging. Here are some things to remind yourself:

More Mental Messages to Boost Your Confidence

1. The audience is here because they are interested in my subject. They *want* to like me. They did not come here to watch me fail.

2. I am well prepared. I may not have the last word on the issue, but what I do have to say is carefully considered and well documented.

3. I'm not planning to revolutionize anyone's way of thinking. If a few people come away with some new ideas and feel better about themselves and their options, then I have accomplished something worthwhile.

4. Some people may disagree with me. Everyone is entitled to his own opinion. You can't please everyone.

5. Some people may actually dislike me. How petty of them. I guess I can live with it.

6. Even if this presentation doesn't go as well as I'd hoped, I will be better for having done it. If I make some mistakes, I'll know what to do differently next time.

You gain something from every presentation you give. If it goes well, you feel a notch more competent. If it doesn't, you decide, "I'll know what to avoid in the future!" Either way, it's a learning experience.

Every learning experience, success or failure, bolsters your confidence. Each presentation becomes a little easier. You may never get over feeling nervous, but if you anticipate it, you can learn to control it.

As Jeanne McClaran tells her clients: "You don't want the butterflies to go away. You want them to fly in formation!"

Chapter Fifteen

Tricks of the Acting Trade

As a workshop leader, you play several roles: content expert, teacher, facilitator, performer. You may not think of yourself as a performer, not in the class of Sammy Davis, Jr., or Barbra Streisand, but after you've conducted the same workshop a dozen or more times, you begin to feel like one. Like an actor reciting from a script, you've planned what you're going to say and rehearsed it so that it will sound spontaneous. If the audience responds positively, you'll lock it into your repertoire forever.

The better your presentation, the more often you'll be asked to repeat it. Someone will call you and say, "I heard about that great talk you gave to the Realtors Association. Would you be willing to put on the same program for our Independent Business Owners group?"

And of course you're delighted. That's the reason you invested so much time in designing and refining the program materials and format. Now the effort pays off. You don't have to spend several days researching a new topic. You just plug in and turn yourself on like a videotape playback.

Or do you?

Now the challenge is: How do you avoid *sounding* like a tape recording? How do you make the material sound as fresh the fiftieth time as the first time you said it?

TRICKS OF THE ACTING TRADE

Robert L. Burpee offers some solutions in his unique workshop, "Speaking as a Performing Art." The two-day program shows how to use acting techniques—vocal variety, facial expressions, and body language—to pump life into a presentation and captivate an audience. Burpee also helps participants turn nervousness into positive energy and to come across as more interesting, effective communicators.

The program was originally designed for school teachers, who know well the difficulty of covering the same lessons over and over, year after year, without sounding boring or bored. Burpee can relate to the problem. He was once a bored teacher himself.

The thing is, Bob Burpee planned to be an actor, not a teacher. He earned a teaching certificate because it was part of his college's graduation requirements, and set out for the Royal Scottish Academy of Music and Dramatic Arts. Impressive, huh? The credential filled half the page of his resume. But when he returned to the States, he found that "opportunities in the acting profession make the teaching profession look very, very lucrative."

He learned a lot at the academy in Scotland, but even more at the hands of his junior high students. After a rather dismal first year, he began to draw on what he had learned as an actor to generate more enthusiasm in the classroom. "Acting is much like teaching. In both cases you're trying to 'sell' an idea," he points out. As he became more animated, the students became more responsive, and—surprise—he began to really *like* teaching! He also concluded, "If you can hold the attention of a seventh grader, you can do anything!"

Some teachers approached him for pointers on how to use drama in the classroom. They were interested in putting on plays and skits and the like. But Burpee realized that

what the teachers needed first was an orientation to basic acting techniques so that they could release some of their own inhibitions and put their ideas across more effectively.

Think about the teachers you admired most in school. The most effective teachers exuded warmth and enthusiasm. They came across as authorities but at the same time, as human beings whom you could relate to.

Now think about your worst teachers. They probably paced around nervously or stood stock still, speaking in a monotone. They read from a pile of notes during the entire class period, or perhaps turned their backs to you and wrote on the blackboard. If anyone asked a question, they looked impatient.

You remember the way these teachers acted. You probably don't remember a thing they taught you.

Almost by accident, Burpee's workshop evolved to fill an un-met—in fact, previously undiscovered—need. Teachers who used to receive consistently low ratings from their students—"bor-ing," "treats me like a number"—began getting positive re-views. With more self-confidence, the teachers became even more effective. Enthusiasm, he points out, feeds on itself.

Word spread, and Burpee's "platform skills" workshop be-gan drawing interest from people in other professions—sales, politics, public relations, training and development. His partici-pants have ranged from an opera singer, to a social worker who counsels unwed mothers, to an ambulance driver faced with keeping people calm in emergencies.

"Good communication skills are the same," he believes, "whether you are talking 1 on 1 to another individual; 1 on 20 at a staff meeting, or 1 on 500 in a public address."

LOOSEN UP, LIVEN UP

Bob Burpee's workshop runs two full days and is limited to 12 participants. That way he can give each one plenty of personal-ized attention, including videotaped feedback of his or her speak-ing performance. This is no lay-back-and-listen session. "I lecture at the beginning to explain some general concepts, but then they start putting them into practice," he says. "They do all the work—physical movement, vocal exercises, interpretive readings. The room ends up smelling like a gymnasium. At the end of the day, people are exhausted."

He flashes back to the training he received in acting school. "At the Royal Academy, we learned to look at performance from a very technical perspective; to break down body and voice into different components. You focus on enunciation, tone and speed of speaking; on your posture and carriage; on the way you use your hands to put a point across. You develop your physical abil-ities much as a professional athlete would."

He cites a college study of how adults learn:

The researchers found that people retain 10 percent of what they read; 20 percent of what they hear; 40 percent of what they see and hear; and up to 90 percent of what they do themselves. Thus, the most effective workshop gives people hands-on experience and practice.

That's why I go for a very animated, participative presenta-tion. The more of your senses I can engage—eyes, ears and body—the more likely it is that you will remember my mes-sage.

"A workshop is like theater to me," he continues.

> People become all of one mind, all focused on the same thing. For the time that we're together, we've all touched one another in some way. We've shared an experience.
>
> Actors are great thieves. When we see something we like, we grab it and store it away in our brain and pull it out again whenever we need it. If it helps get your message across, use it.

Develop your own observation skills, he advises. The next time you're listening to a boring lecture or after-dinner speech, instead of letting your mind drift, ask yourself: What is the speaker doing that is driving me crazy? When you're watching the network news, pay attention to the *way* the newscasters speak. Listen to their vocal quality, their intonation and pacing. When they are doing something right, pick it apart. What are they doing that is so captivating?

"I frankly believe that there is nothing original about any of us," Burpee concludes. "We're the sum total of everyone we've ever met. Consciously or unconsciously, we pick up traits from other people. So I'm saying, be selective! Do it consciously!"

A MANNER OF SPEAKING

"The problem people have with public speaking is that they are so content-oriented, so absorbed in what they are saying that they ignore the importance of *how they say it*. People won't remember diddly-squat of your message if they are distracted by a monotonous voice or nervous mannerisms," Bob Burpee believes. He tells the following story about a college professor with a habit practically everyone will recognize.

> He was considered one of the star faculty members on campus, a leader in his field. But none of us students ever learned anything from him and he never realized it.
>
> He was a teacher who, um, tended to um, say, "um," quite a bit while he was, um, talking.
>
> *He* probably thought he was fascinating, because while he was lecturing, all of the students appeared to be furiously taking notes. We weren't, of course. We were counting the number of times he said "um." After class each day, we compared tallies. Once he said "um" 600 times during the course of a two hour lecture!

"Um" isn't the only habit you have to look out for. A well-timed smile, a pause, a physical gesture can accentuate one of your major points and rivet it in the minds of your audience. On the other hand, unsuitable facial, vocal, or body expressions can so thoroughly distract their attention that they won't remember any of the content of your speech. They will only remember that you paced about the stage like an expectant father or waved your hands like a windmill.

From Bob Burpee and other experts, here's more advice:

Hands.   Gestures with your hands should be smooth and fluid. They should reinforce your message, not flutter about aimlessly. Many of us are plenty nervous when we go up before an audience, and all that nervous energy seems to get released through our fingertips; our hands go like airplane propellors. But the only message they reinforce is agitation and discomfort.

How can you control your hands? Don't lock them behind your back, as if bound by a straitjacket. And don't thrust them into the pockets of your jacket. Rather than striking a relaxed pose, you'll look like you're gripping a concealed weapon. Instead, give those hands something to do. Put a pencil in one of them, a pointer or even your lecture notes.

Feet.   Question: What can be worse than a speaker who stands stock still, as if her shoes are glued to the floor boards? Answer: One who paces back and forth like a duck in a shooting gallery.

If you are standing at a lectern, plant your feet about 12 inches part, one a bit in front of the other. This will keep you from rocking back and forth on your heels. Then once you've gotten your bearings, relax and move around a bit. Again, *meaningful* movement provides a release of nervous energy and holds the audience's attention.

Trainer Ken Jones says, "I never remain standing in front of the audience when I am giving a training session. I move from table to table, sometimes speaking from the middle of the group, sometimes from the back of the room. It establishes a better rapport with the audience. I'm part of the group, not some wooden authority figure up next to the blackboard." Dean Osterman agrees: "When a speaker moves around it keeps things from getting static. It discourages participants from exchanging comments while I'm talking. They never know where I'm going to pop up next!"

Posture.   Do you slouch? Do you speak with your head modestly bowed? Then you are inadvertently creating an impression of inadequacy and inferiority (to say nothing of a double chin!). If you are doing it advertently, for heaven's sake, why? This is no time for humility. Meekness conveys weakness. These people are present to hear an expert! Don't disappoint them. The more you act like one, the more you'll be treated like one. And inevitably, you'll begin to feel like one.

Eye contact.   Remember your high school speech class? The teacher probably advised you to focus your eyes just above the audience—perhaps on the heating vent in the back of the room. The idea was, since the audience makes you nervous, pretend it isn't there. Nonsense. How can you communicate without making eye contact?

Your audience's facial expressions will tell you instantly whether you are belaboring a point or moving too quickly. You need this feedback. In a small group of a dozen or 20, you can meet the eyes of each person in the room during your talk. Speaking before a large audience, you can still create the feeling of touching each person directly by focusing on a few specific people in various parts of the audience. Sweep your eyes slowly, don't throw darting glances. Be sure to take in the persons seated off to one side and the group in the back rows.

Speakers often avoid looking directly at the audience for fear of seeing a face that looks bored or critical. For every one of those, you'll find 10 others nodding at you in agreement.

Pitch and pacing.   Your voice is a very versatile instrument. You can vary the volume, the high and low notes, the speed and the strength to express feelings and emotion. Listen to your voice on a tape recorder. If you have a tendency to drone, practice varying the pitch and tone of your delivery. Pump some enthusiasm into it.

If   you   talk   too   slowly   you   will put   people   to   sleep. Ontheotherhandifyoutalktoo-rapidlynoonewillbeabletofollowwhatyouaresaying. You're aiming for a normal conversational tone and, for most people, that's about 175 words per minute. You can test yourself by reading aloud from this book and counting the number of words you cover in 60 seconds. Did you surpass 200? Slow down, or you'll risk sounding like a machine gun. Less than 150? Rev up, or you may lull people to sleep. *Pace* your delivery. Accentuate the points you feel are most important. Pause for a couple of seconds. Let them sink in.

"Failure to pause is a very common mistake," says speech

consultant Jeanne L. McClaran. "Many speakers feel they must keep up a running stream of words, filling up every millisecond with "ums." If they only knew how much better it would be to say *nothing*. A spoken message is like a printed message. The key points are conveyed more effectively if they are surrounded by white space."

Empty phrases.   To make your message come across with vitality and conviction, avoid conditional terms like "kind of," "sort of," and "maybe." They dilute your message and make you sound uncertain and wishy-washy.

And while we're on the subject of "filler" words, make every effort to remove "y'know" from your vocabulary. It makes you sound insecure about what you're saying, y'know? And don't punctuate every sentence with "okay," okay?

Other assorted quirks.   You may or may not be aware of them. Your family has learned to put up with them, even tune them out ... those little nervous mannerisms like sucking your teeth, stroking your beard, tugging your ear, cracking your knuckles. But to an audience, they are magnified twenty-fold. You could be offering your audience free hundred dollar bills, and they would not react. They are transfixed by your bad habits.

GET SOME FEEDBACK

See yourself as others see you. If you live near a large city or a college campus, see if you can hire someone to videotape one of your presentations. Many workshops in public speaking, like Bob Burpee's program, offer video-recording sessions so that you can practice in front of a camera and then see an instant replay. If you have such an opportunity, take advantage of it.

Then brace yourself. On the TV screen, all of your physical imperfections are magnified (especially to you, the nonimpartial observer). Your crooked tooth looks like a walrus tusk. You look fat; the camera always seems to add at least 10 pounds to everyone's appearance. Try to look past these minor flaws. This isn't a screen test. Nobody ever said that to be an effective teacher, you have to rival Victoria Principal or Tom Selleck.

It's the voice, gestures, mannerisms, physical movement you need to examine. These are the things you can change, with practice.

If you don't have access to video equipment, borrow a cassette tape recorder and unobtrusively record your voice while you are speaking. Later you can evaluate your verbal delivery for pitch, pacing, clarity, and general effectiveness.

I think that the best of all feedback devices is another person . . . a friend or colleague who can observe you as you are talking and come back with constructive criticism. A machine can only tell it like it is. A live person can *interpret* what you're doing right and wrong and suggest ways for you to improve. Choose your critic carefully. Someone who can be honest and objective, and who won't feel constrained by a fear of hurting your feelings. A spouse is not a good candidate.

Ask the person who helps you to notice your strengths as well as your weaknesses. The objective is to improve your presentation style, not destroy your confidence. The checklist in Appendix D should help.

Ideally, you want to reach the point where you are no longer concerned about your face, your voice, and your physical appearance at all. You care only about your audience, and they can tell.

Chapter Sixteen

Promotion and Marketing

Promotion and marketing are to your workshop what propellors are to a plane. Without them, it will never fly. It won't even get off the ground.

It doesn't matter that you're a riveting speaker or that your subject matter is momentous. If nobody hears about you, nobody's going to come.

Does this mean that you launch your adult education venture with a full page ad in *The New York Times?* Of course not. The most prudent marketing approach might be captioned: "Test before you invest." Advertise your seminar locally and measure the response. If you seem to have tapped a real need, start spreading the word on a wider scale.

PHASE ONE: SENDING UP A TRIAL BALLOON

Dorothy Lemkuhl did this; she sent her trial balloon aloft before completely committing herself. As the idea for her popular "Clutterbug" course on home organizing was taking shape in her mind, she began talking it up among friends and asking what they thought of the idea. When the unanimous response was "Where do I sign up?" she knew she was on to something. Author Christine Liu gave her first workshops on "Nutritional Chinese Cooking" in her own kitchen, among people she knew. She has gone on to publish three cookbooks and makes numerous public appearances. Her cooking demonstrations serve as an effective means of promoting the books, and vice versa.

121

I conducted my first time management workshop on a Saturday morning in my own living room. But rather than rounding up a dozen close friends, I invited people who agreed to be candid—even critical—in evaluating the content of the program and my presentation skills. This test run provided valuable feedback. In their evaluations, the group told me which parts of the workshop they found most interesting and suggested other topics that could be shortened or dropped from the format. They praised my "great rapport with the audience" but said I'd better learn to do something with my hands. Overall, the response was encouraging. The consensus was, "This is pretty good. Here's how you can make it better."

PHASE TWO: GAINING SPONSORSHIP

Once you have tested your program and gained confidence, you could go out and promote your own local seminar. But that requires capital—at least $500 for printing up brochures, reserving a meeting space, and publicizing the event. As an interim strategy, why not sign on with one of the adult education programs in your community?

If you live in a large metropolitan area, you'll probably find a number of options—the public school system, city recreation department, a local community college, the 'Y', or one of the growing number of noncredit adult learning networks. Which ones seem to have the largest following? What services do they provide for teachers and students? Which ones offer programming that would be most compatible with yours?

Even though your association will be relatively informal, it will give you added visibility and credentials. It makes sense to affiliate with an organization with an excellent reputation and an aggressive marketing program. In addition, you may find that some community colleges and college extension services confer titles like "faculty associate." This will certainly look nice on your resume.

Once you choose an organization you'd like to link up with, it, of course, must accept you. But this may be the easy part. Noncredit-programming coordinators are always on the lookout for new and interesting courses. Most will pay you an hourly fee or a percentage of the tuition. If the number of enrollees isn't sufficient to meet the program's expenses, it will be canceled. From the sponsor's point of view, there's little risk in including you in its catalogue and seeing what kind of response your course brings.

When you make an appointment with the director of your local adult learning organization, prepare as you would for a job interview. Bring a written outline of your subject matter, examples of any handout materials you have prepared, and a copy of your resume or bio sheet. And don't suppress your enthusiasm. It's your strongest selling point.

In the future, you may be holding similar meetings with corporate administrators who want to hire you to conduct inservice training sessions or book you for an upcoming conference. This interview will give you good practice in promoting your program.

Associating with an adult education organization of some kind offers you other advantages:

- You get free publicity. Your name and program description appear on a flyer or in a course catalogue that is widely circulated.
- The organization arranges for facilities, handles registration and other logistics, freeing you to concentrate on teaching.
- You become part of a network of free-lance teachers, with whom you can exchange ideas and mutual support.

PHASE THREE: MOUNTING YOUR OWN WORKSHOP

Producing your own workshop under your own business name can be professionally and financially rewarding. It marks your transition from hobbyist to entrepreneur. If you have carefully researched the market, identified a need, and put together a first-rate program, you are indeed ready for this step.

Your first independently produced seminar is, in itself, a marketing tool. If it's good, word will spread, and the very best kind of publicity is word-of-mouth. As your reputation grows, the demand for your services will become self-sustaining.

So right from the start, establish yourself as a class act. Don't be tempted to cut corners by renting inferior meeting space in a no-name hotel, or by typing up your own brochure. When people learn about your program, their first impression should be "quality"—not "bargain."

You should anticipate the following start-up expenses:

Printing (brochures, flyers, business cards, stationery, and envelopes)

Postage (possibly including a bulk-rate mailing permit)

Telephone (and maybe an answering service)

Meeting room rental

Coffee and other refreshments

Advertising and publicity

Copying costs for handout materials

Miscellaneous supplies (folders, name tags, pencils, felt-tip markers, newsprint chart, etc.)

Eventually you may anticipate other costs such as office rental and hired assistants. But that can wait until after you start turning a large profit.

DESIGNING A BROCHURE

If you are preparing to put on a seminar under your own business name, one of the first things you'll need is a professional-looking, eye-catching brochure to provide information and, especially, to convince people to come. But you should consider devising a brochure even if you're not planning a specific event. This could be a one-page flyer describing the program content, your qualifications as instructor, and possibly including a list of organizations that have sent representatives to previous programs. If a company wants to hire you as a consultant and asks, "Can you send me something that describes your workshop?" you assure them you can, and pop the brochure in the mail.

This piece of paper is the first contact many people will have with your program, so it must make an immediate, positive impression. In many cases, it will be the factor deciding whether they will attend your program or hire you as a consultant, so it is worth all the time and attention you can give to it.

You don't need to spend a fortune on a slick, four-color brochure that unfolds like a road map. But neither should you make do with a single page run off by a mimeograph machine. A brochure is a reflection of the workshop itself, so it should project—

- Authority
- Imagination
- Substance

Above all, it should communicate quality. Spend a little extra for professional typesetting and design work. Have it printed or photocopied on cover stock paper. There's a lot of reading material out there vying for people's attention. Yours has to immediately say, "This is of interest! Read me!"

"Beginning with the title, right through to the registration form at the end, all copy should be written in terms of benefits to the attendee," stresses Kathryn S. Collins, director of the Institute for Professional Businesswomen, a division of Fred Pryor, Inc. "We [workshop promoters] tend to tell what our program is about rather than describing what our program can do for the attendee."

> For example, we say, "During this workshop, the steps for giving an effective presentation will be analyzed." That's telling them *about* our program. Benefit copy might read: "You'll feel more confident about your presentation when you know the six steps of successful speaking."
>
> Careful use of space, line and color can "lead" readers through the copy, causing them to focus on the most important points.[1]

The brochure layout serves this function. One of the most versatile formats is the three- or four-panel foldout that can be mailed alone or enclosed in a standard business envelope. The end panel is reserved for a tearoff registration form and another panel is left blank for the address.

Study a few of the brochures that you receive in the mail and see how they're put together. What makes them attractive and readable? What ideas might you adapt for your own product? Examine them for style and content.

Your brochure should answer the following questions for readers:

What's the purpose of this program?

Why should I attend?

What will I learn?

How long will it take?

Who is the teacher?

How will I benefit?

If the brochure is promoting a specific, scheduled workshop, it must also answer:

When will it be held?

Where will it be held?

---

[1]Kathryn S. Collins, "Why Should I Read This?" *The Learning Connection*, May 1984, p. 2.

How much does it cost?

How do I register?

You can view each of these segments of information like pieces of a puzzle. They can be moved about, played up or down, to suit your needs. Some can be omitted. Here's what you've got to work with:

What Goes into a Brochure

1. *Attention grabbers.* This may be a question, phrase, illustration—anything that causes the recipient to take notice and read on.

2. *Workshop title.* It may be catchy or straightforward (see Appendix B), but it should be specific.

3. *Description.* A short paragraph or outline highlights the issues to be addressed and/or topics to be covered. It answers the question, "What will I learn?" Some brochures simply include the program agenda.

4. *Who should attend.* Is your workshop specifically designed for: New managers? Trade unionists? Clerical workers? Career changers? Identify your target audience. If it has broad, general appeal, make that clear with a phrase like, "Educators, business professionals, homemakers, and students can all benefit from this program."

5. *Workshop leader(s).* A brief paragraph on you and your co–presenters, if any, should summarize the credentials that are relevant to the workshop theme. A photo is optional.

6. *Benefits.* What new skills or capabilities will people gain from attending? What results can they expect? Be as specific as possible.

7. *Comments from past participants.* Include testimonials that cite benefits and express high enthusiasm. These can be attributed to a named person, to an occupational type (i.e., "retired accountant"), or they may just appear as unattributed quotes.

8. *Partial list of organizations that have sponsored your program or sent participants.* Include only prestigious, recognized groups and companies.

9. *Handouts.* Does your program provide special handout materials, such as a resource notebook? If so, describe it, or mention it with "benefits."

If the brochure is for a specific event, don't forget to include the following:

10. *Time, date, and place.* Add a simple map if needed.

11. *Registration procedure.* Are you taking registration by mail, phone, or at the door? Do you accept credit cards? Is there a discount for two or more persons from the same company? What's your cancellation and refund policy?

12. *Tax deduction.* Continuing education expenses, including registration fees, travel, lodging, and meals, to "maintain and improve professional skills" are tax deductible. If your program qualifies, indicate this on your brochure.

13. *Registration form.* Include space for the person's name, organization, title, address, and telephone number. In laying out your brochure, be certain the other side of the mail-in form does not contain information that is pertinent to the attendee (such as the date and location, or your phone number.)

14. *Can't attend?* Invite the reader to be added to your mailing list. This option could be included as a checkoff on your registration form.

15. *Act now!* Provide the reader with an incentive to register before motivation wanes. Offer a discount for registering in advance, or add a statement such as: "Enroll early. Attendance is strictly limited to ensure maximum individualized instruction."

BE YOUR OWN PRESS AGENT

Now that you have your brochures, to whom do you send them? With postage rates at a premium, you'll want to target them, as directly as possible, to people who are most likely to attend. You know they're out there. Here are some ways to reach them.

Direct Mail

Send the brochure to everyone you know, or to anyone who might be someone who would be interested. Scribble a personal note in the margin. Mail two, adding the request: "Please post this on the office bulletin board," or "Pass along the extra copy to a friend."

Over time, you'll build a mailing list of everyone who has ever attended one of your workshops, or even inquired about them. Trade lists with other seminar sponsors. People who have attended other programs may be likely candidates for yours.

Should you buy or rent a mailing list? Yes, *if* the target audience is one that is easily distinguished by occupation, academic degree, or common interest. Thousands of direct-mail marketing lists are available: magazine subscriber lists, organization membership rosters, household census lists. And these can get very specific, even down to "everyone in Arizona who bought a recreational vehicle during the past year."

So, if the workshop is for new business owners, you might get a good response from the subscribers to *Inc. Magazine*. If it is a workshop for lawyers, direct your mailing to members of the state bar association.

Most lists are broken down by geographic area or zip code, so you can target persons who live within reasonable driving distance of your event. A central resource for information on more than 25,000 direct-mail marketing lists is:

Standard Rates and Data Service
3004 Glenview Road
Wilmette, Illinois 60091

What kind of response rate can you expect from direct mail? Most professional promoters count on 0.5 to 1.0 percent, and anything over 2 percent is considered exceptional. Thus, to fill a room with 30 people, you'd better plan to send out at least 5000 brochures.

In this league, it pays to buy a bulk-mailing permit. But remember, third-class bulk mail is treated as low priority. Depending upon the time of year, mail volume, and other factors, the Post Office recommends allowing up to three or more weeks for delivery. One of the most common mistakes of amateur publicists is sending out announcements by third-class mail a mere two weeks ahead of time—and having them arrive *after* the event!

Advertising

Direct mail marketing works best when you have a well-defined audience, such as "mathematics teachers living within a 50-mile radius of Madison, Wisconsin, who are involved in computer-assisted instruction." But what if your workshop is on a very general topic, like "Improving Personal Relationships?" A mass mailing is about as practical as dropping leaflets from an airplane. A newspaper display ad may be more cost effective.

Generally speaking, a display ad will carry much of the same information as your brochure:

- Headline, to grab the reader's attention.
- Outline or summary of the workshop contents (stressing the benefits to participants).

- Presenter(s) and credentials.
- Time, date, location, and fee.
- Registration procedure—either your address and phone number or a clipout form. If you accept credit cards, list which ones.
- An inducement for the reader to "act now!" Induce them to call or write immediately before turning the page and losing interest.

The disadvantage to display advertising is that large ads are expensive and small ones may go unnoticed. Many newspapers will not guarantee the spot where the ad will be placed, or will charge extra for "preferred placement." If you are offered a choice of placement, go for the local news section, not the obituary page.

Classified ads are another alternative. Far less expensive than display copy, these tiny ads may put you in direct contact with your most receptive audience. A seminar on real estate investments, for example, would attract attention under the "Business Opportunities" column. A workshop on resume writing could be advertised under "Help Wanted."

Your classified ad needn't be lengthy. Just a sentence or two, with a phone number, can enable you to gauge interest. Frances Davis, a retired social worker, ran a "tickler ad" under the general employment section that read, "Homemakers: ready to reenter the job market? Call [phone number]." The response was high enough to convince her to teach a workshop on job reentry skills.

Press Coverage

Newspaper editors and reporters can be valuable allies in conveying your message to the public. If your program is newsworthy, and if you supply the information in the right format to the right person, and carefullly observe deadlines, most newspapers will be very cooperative in publicizing your event.

Strategy 1. Write your own press release. Editors are always busy and under pressure, so make their job as easy as possible. Type up the basic who, what, when, where, and why of your event and direct it to the proper person (the women's news editor, the business editor, etc.) who covers news related to your area. Keep the item brief. (See Appendix E for a model press release.) If you expect to be dealing with this editor on a continuing basis, make it a point to introduce yourself and establish personal contact.

Strategy 2. Invite the editor or writer to attend the workshop as your guest. It's good public relations, and may net you an article. Not only will this be good visibility when it appears, but the reprints will be an impressive addition to your promotional materials.

Strategy 3.   Offer to be interviewed on your subject matter, suggesting some timely or provocative angle. (For instance, the holidays can be stressful as well as enjoyable. As a family therapist who conducts seminars on parenting, you can offer some tips on ways to cope with the extra financial and social pressures of the season.)

Strategy 4.   Write a letter to the editor on some subject that reflects your expertise. ("As a Red Cross volunteer, I'd like to call the public's attention to our fall series of preventive health care classes . . .")

Finally, don't overlook ongoing feature articles like community-happenings columns or events calendars. Check ahead. Many weekly columns have early deadlines.

Radio

Many radio stations sponsor live interview shows and community forums. The producers of these shows are constantly on the lookout for newsworthy speakers and subject matter. Try to get a booking on such a show a week or two before your workshop. The host or hostess won't mind giving your upcoming program a plug if it represents news of interest to the public. Supply sample questions in advance to ensure that you have an opportunity to convey the desired message.

Most radio stations will also be willing to broadcast PSAs (public service announcements) for the programs you conduct for public or nonprofit organizations. To submit PSAs, type up three versions of your workshop announcement (on letterhead stationery) that can be read aloud within 10, 15, and 20 seconds. (See Appendix F for a sample.) Call the station and get the name of the "community programming director" (or similar title) so you can direct the copy to the right person. Many radio stations log PSAs one month in advance, so be sure to submit the material well ahead of this deadline.

Television

Johnny Carson may be a long shot. But your local cable access channels or public broadcasting stations may be happy to book you for their local "Business Beat" or "Community Showcase" programs. Don't discount these local variety or talk shows. There's no quicker way to achieve name recognition and celebrity status. And except for your investment of time, it's free publicity.

Television stations also allocate time for public service announcements. To find out procedures for submitting information, contact the station and ask to speak with the person in charge of community service or public affairs. As with newspapers and radio, if you submit the information on time and according to specifications, the chances are good that you'll get air time—even though it may be slotted toward the end of "Midnight Movie."

Spread the Word

Is your workshop of interest to members of local civic associations, business associations, women's groups? Contact the presidents of these organizations and ask if your event can be announced at the next meeting. Offer to drop off copies of the brochure. If you will be attending the meeting, you can make the announcement yourself.

Check with the Chamber of Commerce to see what conferences are being held in your community. Obtain permission to leave a stack of brochures on the conference-literature display table.

Accept all offers of speaking engagements, including groups that can't pay an honorarium. The key themes of your presentation can be easily recast into a 20-minute after-dinner speech, and you get a free plug in the meeting notice that appears in the newspaper. Each member of the audience is a potential client or a catalyst for future bookings.

To promote a relatively high-priced or longer series of classes, offer a "free introductory session." At this meeting you can share some insights and preview the topics to be covered during the subsequent longer course. Make this talk instructive—not merely a sales pitch. You might give the audience a quiz, designed to point up their need for the full program. Offer a discount to anyone who signs up that night.

When members of your audience say they enjoyed your presentation, encourage them to tell others. And when program sponsors send you a glowing thank-you letter, make photocopies and include them with your promotional materials. Personal referrals are the best, most credible publicity you can get.

And finally, don't be too shy about talking up your program yourself. There's no shame in being enthusiastic about something you've worked hard to make a success. You have to blow your own horn a little bit if you want others to pick up the tune.

Chapter Seventeen

Are You Ready for the Big Time?

In the course of this book, I've presented interviews of many newcomers to the workshop business to show you how to get started. To bring the book full circle, it seemed I should talk to a typical pro, someone who is pursuing this profession on a national scale, someone whose personal career path might serve as a model for readers of this book.

Still, there's nothing "typical" about Larry Kokkelenberg.

Most people reach the national seminar circuit by way of the corporate ladder. Kokkelenberg started out in social work. With a bachelor's degree in sociology, he first worked as a community organizer in Chicago. He earned his Master's in Social Work and began doing clinical group counseling and therapy, working with some individuals who were deeply emotionally disturbed. An unpretentious, compassionate man, he built up a considerable practice and reputation in the Chicago area.

But he became dissatisfied with "impacting people one at a time." He began training others in his clinical and counseling methods—ministers, physicians, psychologists—and some of this work overlapped into business consulting. He returned to school again—this time for a Ph.D. in clinical and industrial psychology, and began building an impressive clientele list: the U.S. Civil Service Commission, the U.S. Army, Owens Corning Fiberglass, Honeywell, IBM.

At age 40, he is one of about 40 independent faculty members for Associated Management Institute (AMI) and president of his own firm in Chicago, Kokkelenberg Corporation. He consults in all areas of human resources, specializing in needs analysis, conflict resolution, team building, and minimizing the problems of employee turnover and organizational change.

It all comes back to helping people, whether it's on an individual or organization-wide basis.

On the day of our interview, the brochure bills him as Lawrence D. Kokkelenberg, Ph.D., in town to present one of the AMI series of management seminars at the Airport Sheraton before an assortment of administrators and executives. But if you're expecting someone in a three-piece suit reciting organizational theory and academic jargon, Kokkelenberg breaks the mold again. He looks almost collegiate in a red tie and navy blue blazer. What's really out of sync is the cast and crutches.

"One of my goals was to go skiing at least four tims this winter," he informs the group cheerfully. He taps his broken ankle with one crutch. "This goal will have to be on hold for a few months."

His message to the 25 assembled participants: Be very goal oriented, but be flexible. Keep reassessing your plans. If something goes wrong, shift gears.

I had wondered how a nationally promoted AMI seminar at $200 per person might differ from the garden variety workshop at $35 per person mounted by the local community education department. Would there be caviar for midmorning break? A live floor show? It turns out that the audio-visuals and teaching format are not very different from what you'd find in the average workshop—a mixture of lecture, workbook exercises, and small group discussions.

What makes this seminar above average is Kokkelenberg himself. He knows how to pace the material and "read" the group, giving us lots of information but also an opportunity to process it. He weaves in personal opinions and anecdotes that the group—who cover a wide range of backgrounds and job levels—can relate to. He has given this material hundreds of times, to over 30,000 people by his own estimate, yet there's no hint that he's bored by it.

"You need a good theoretical base and a good command of the subject," he observes in our conversation after the seminar. "You need an interesting subject to begin with. And you need some practical experience to make it real."

"But anyone can stand up in front of a group and deliver data," he continues. "I honestly believe that anyone in that seminar today could have done what I did. The added dimension is that you have to care about it. That's what comes through to the audience—that you're a sensitive, caring person."

One of the things he prides himself on is the ability to present a workshop to a group of construction foremen one day and a team of nuclear physicists the next. It takes different approaches to relate to each group, but he seems to make the transition effortlessly.

"You can never become overconfident in this business, because if you did, you'd stop trying to improve. But you need a strong enough ego to be able to forget about yourself." He explains:

> I have a colleague who hasn't reached that point yet. She's very knowledgeable in her subject; but when she speaks, she is worrying, "What do they think of me? How am I coming across?" If anyone is critical of the seminar, she takes it personally. You can't do that. You can't give your best to the audience if you're wrapped up in yourself.

But that's not to say he doesn't care what people think of him. Kokkelenberg sets very high standards for himself. He expects the great majority of his evaluations to be marked "outstanding," and when someone rates him "satisfactory"—a rare occurrence—he feels that he has failed that person.

Success in training and consulting has only whetted his appetite for new challenges. Two years ago, Kokkelenberg began operating a small paving and asphalt contracting business, and recently he started a truck-leasing firm. Why? Partly to see if he could succeed at it. It's the same rationale that fuels his off-hours pursuits: white water canoeing, flying, and skiing in downhill races.

The broken ankle? He doesn't view it as a penalty for taking risks, but another challenge. You think it's tiring to be on your feet teaching for eight hours? Try doing it on one foot!

Try maneuvering in and out of hotels and airports with the briefcase and luggage. Yet you have the feeling Kokkelenberg didn't reduce his schedule any because of his skiing mishap. Says Kokkelenberg, "I enjoy some of the travel, the level of income and the freedom. What I dislike most is not the jet lag. It's the fact that I might get to know someone in a seminar quite well, discover we have much in common, and know that I will never see them again."

Balancing that is what he calls "the lack of responsibility"—that is, no more 3 A.M. phone calls from suicidal clients. "My responsibility after this seminar is to be in Chicago by 3 P.M. tomorrow, and that's it. I have 18 hours to make plane connections. I know I can handle that."

He currently travels about 40 days per year for his own company and 110 for AMI, which he calls "one of the best seminar organizations in the country."

"AMI acts as a broker and marketing agent," he explains. "The company, which calls itself 'a nonprofit educational corporation' has spent over $3 million merging and purging its mailing lists, so it is extremely effective at targeting its audience. Every seminar organization in the country except AMI lost money in 1981, and 11 went out of business."

An independent faculty member may be paid $600 to $1200 per day plus travel and other expenses presenting a program for an organization such as AMI. Should you shoot for the moon and send in your resume? "AMI receives about 300 applications each year and they all look good," Kokkelenberg observes. "University professors, business school faculty who look at the seminar circuit and think, what a great way to make a little extra income. It's extremely competitive.

"But sure, send in your resume. What have you got to lose?"

Chapter Eighteen

A Talk with Danny Simon

A continuing theme of this book is that to break into the workshop business, you do not have to be awesomely talented or world famous. Some of the most successful teachers—the vast majority in fact—are men and women with ordinary backgrounds and interests. They could be your next-door neighbors or second cousins.

Now meet Danny Simon. He's one of a kind.

A top Hollywood television writer, network and stage director, and sometimes actor, Simon has been teaching his three-day workshop on "The Craft of Comedy Writing for Television" since 1980 at cities and college campuses across the country. He bills the program as an overview of the business since it explores many facets, from simple jokes through the development of sketches and scripts for all forms of variety shows and situation comedies.

For 35 years he has written for the best of them: standup comedians like Milton Berle, Victor Borge, Buddy Hackett, and Phil Silvers; early variety programs such as Sid Caesar's "Show of Shows" and "The Colgate Comedy Hour"; dozens of situation comedies including "Bachelor Father," "McHale's Navy," and "The Real McCoys," and more recently, "One Day at a Time," "The Facts of Life," and "Diff'rent Strokes."

He says he never thought of himself as a teacher, although as head writer for many of those shows he coached dozens of beginning writers including a 17-year-old Woody Allen. Allen is quoted on Simon's workshop program:

I've learned a few things on my own since and modified some
of the things he taught me, but everything, unequivocally,
that I learned about comedy writing, I learned from Danny
Simon.

His kid brother, playwright Neil Simon, also acknowledged the
debt during a 1976 appearance on "Bob Hope's World of Comedy": ". . . No, Bob, I don't think it's possible for someone to teach
anyone else how to write funny.—No, wrong, I think perhaps
there is *one* person who can. My brother Danny. He taught Woody
Allen and he taught me."

I met Danny Simon as his plane landed the evening before
he was to embark on another 20-hour workshop. Even casually
dressed in jeans and a weathered suede jacket, he doesn't project the laid-back leisureliness of his adopted Southern California. He's full of energy. He's still a native New Yorker, with a
quick, broad smile, plenty of candor, and a grousing good humor.
On the drive from the airport to his hotel, he spoke about his
newest profession.

**Q: This is quite a change from your prominent behind-the-
scenes role in show business. How did it get started?**

A: Quite by accident. I was invited by a friend from Universal pictures to address his film class. I didn't go without trepi-
dation. I don't believe I had ever spoken before a group larger
than six people. I wasn't sure I would have anything valuable to
say. To my delight, it went very well. At the end of the class, the
students voted to give up their lunch hour in order to continue
our discussion.

I was asked to give more guest lectures, and on one occasion a *Chicago Tribune* writer came in and audited the class. The
article she wrote was syndicated to other newspapers, and soon
I was getting requests from colleges all over the country. I've had
to limit the programs to one or two per month, in fact. The response has overwhelmed me.

**Q: What do you do in the class? Do you critique the students'
scripts?**

A: No. I have so many things to teach my students that the
time can be better spent on other endeavors. Instead, I focus on
the *technique* of comedy writing so that from here on, for the rest
of their careers, my students can teach themselves. I do this by
working on the thought processes that every writer, in comedy
or drama, must go through in order to develop a script. We actually create the conditions of a typical writers' conference room.

Q: You must limit the class size, then.

A: Yes, it is limited to 40 participants because I take lots of questions and engage them in the discussion. I want to be able to address each person's needs and concerns. If the class is too large, that's not possible.

I've been asked to come up with a correspondence course. They tell me I could make a million dollars. That doesn't interest me. That would be a cheat. There's no way you can teach people to write by a correspondence course. I have to be able to listen to what people have to say; to give them feedback and suggestions, face to face. You can't have that kind of communication with a correspondence course!

Q: You seem to really care about your students.

A: I get very excited when I get very, very bright people. After all, not every comedy writer or potential comedy writer is born in New York or Hollywood. And if I can open doors to these people in some little way, and save them years of trial and error by showing them how to go about their writing, it's very satisfying. I feel like Mr. Chips.

On the other hand, some people will say, you've opened my eyes and shown me that I don't have the right talent, and in those cases, I really have to feel that I am doing these people a service. Why should they waste their time following a fantasy when they may as well be doing something that they are better suited for.

I've always wanted to be a singer, to walk down the street singing, with my coat tossed over my shoulder. . . . What a great life that would be. . . .

Q: Is your class only for aspiring writers?

A: No, in Los Angeles I get many professionals who are on the periphery of the business . . . producers, directors, actors and actresses, as well as actual writers. But as I travel to college campuses around the country, it's mostly people who want to break into comedy writing.

A lot of humor on television today consists of jokes and one-liners. Easy laughs that stop the action. I think good comedy writing is much more than this, and I teach people to focus on the essence of humor, the plot and character development. Using this thought process, students can draw on their own insights and experiences. My students tell me that they can apply these techniques to any kind of writing in any kind of profession.

Q: It sounds as if you adhere to the adage, "Write about what you know."

A: Exactly. The best plays my brother has written are those in which he draws from real life and then exaggerates. Screen-writers are not reporters. We don't write about things exactly as they happen. We perceive a funny situation and then blow it out of proportion.

The play *The Odd Couple* and the way it evolved is an ex-ample. I was working as a writer for the TV series "Make Room for Daddy," recently separated from my wife, and sharing an apartment with a Hollywood agent who had also recently re-turned to bachelorhood. One night we invited friends over for dinner and I cooked a pot roast. It was a fiasco. The dinner burned and we had to make a quick trip to the deli to salvage the evening.

So the next night my friend says to me, "What are we hav-ing for dinner tonight?" And I said, "Dinner! How come you never take me out to dinner! And when was the last time you brought me flowers?!"

That's how the idea of a play about two divorced men, as in-compatible with each other as they had been with their wives, was born. I told Neil about it and he told me it was the greatest idea for a play he had ever heard, and he kept after me to finish it. But I was too involved with my work and other things so I fi-nally said, "Here's the idea; you write it." And the rest is his-tory!

Q: So that's your secret identity. The real-life Felix Unger.

A: Yes, but you see, I'm not as much of a neatnick fuss-budget as Felix, and the agent I was sharing a house with wasn't that much of a slob. It was the exaggeration that made it funny. You pick a believable plot and put in characters with foibles and idiosyncrasies that make them human.

Q: Does conducting workshops conflict with your writing?

A: I really feel that I am a far, far better writer and even a better director than I was three years ago before I began doing this. As a writer, you're only working on one project at a time, and all of your attention is focused on it. But as a teacher, you're discussing the whole amalgam of the entertainment industry. I began to see different factions of the entertainment industry that I had never before taken the time to consider. I'm also meeting lots of interesting people and getting new ideas from them—that's very stimulating.

Now that I've learned all this, I'm looking forward to going back and taking advantage of what I've taught myself.

Q: What has been the most satisfying aspect of this new enterprise?

A: Finding people who remind me of me when I got started ... in the sense that they have a sense of humor and a genuine desire to write. When a student has motivation and true talent, the insights they gain from this course can put them 5 to 10 years ahead of where they would be on their own. The father image in me finds this very satisfying.

Q: Has it changed you?

A: People who come back and take the course a second time tell me that they enjoy seeing my growth as a teacher. I haven't changed my ideas, but I present them in a more organized, systematic way. I'm less dogmatic ... more flexible.

Different jokes for different folks. Comedy is a matter of opinion.

Chapter Nineteen

The Last Word

An earlier chapter referred to this time-honored advice for organizing any oral presentation:

> Tell them what you're going to say.
> Say it.
> Tell them what you said.

The same formula can be applied in books. A closing chapter is like the last page of the flipchart, the final minutes of the workshop. It is a chance to recapitulate the most important points of information and leave you with a few last thoughts. Here goes.

Ten Ways to Insure a Successful Seminar or Workshop

1. Begin with clear objectives. Know what skills can be taught or information conveyed within your allotted time frame.

2. Start planning early. Allow several days for each phase: gathering information; designing the presentation; polishing and rehearsing.

3. Know your audience. Learn all you can in advance about their background and interests, and gear the program directly to them.

4. Check and double check the logistics of your presentation. Visit the facilities; determine the seating arrangements; recheck the equipment, handout materials, visual aids. Leave nothing to chance.

5. Be time conscious. Arrive early; start and end on schedule; follow a prepared agenda; and never go more than 90 minutes without a break.

6. Vary your presentation style with exercises, discussions, and other activities that increase audience involvement.

7. Solicit evaluations from participants so you can make the next workshop even better. If possible, build in a means of followup.

8. Don't be content to learn by trial-and-error. Seek advice from workshop organizers and leaders. Attend their programs; study the way they present information and handle an audience.

9. Keep your sense of humor. You'll need it when (inevitably) something goes wrong.

10. Enjoy yourself. Your enthusiasm is your best teaching asset.

Appendix A

Workshop Leader's Checklist

You've heard of the absent-minded professor? The type of person who is good at designing and teaching a training session is sometimes less efficient at handling room arrangements and organizing supplies. I was fortunate to present some of my first workshops with Charlotte Whitney, who is good at both presentations and preparations.

If you don't have Charlotte, you need her checklist. Before your presentation, be sure you've attended to the following.

AT THE FACILITY:

Lobby sign announcing location of workshop

Coat rack

Lectern

Microphone (if warranted by the size of the group)

Table (for handout materials, book displays)

Comfortable seating with writing surfaces

Ashtrays—if you plan to allow smoking

Coffee or other refreshments

Water pitchers and glasses

Good lighting

Windows and ventilation

Parking accommodations

Restrooms

Registration table

Electrical outlets

PRESENTER'S SUPPLY KIT:

Extra pens, pencils, paper, felt-tip markers

Flipchart and/or newsprint pad

Easel

Audio-visual projector, screen, extra bulbs

Blackboard erasers and extra chalk

Props (for group activities, illustrating points, etc.)

Handout materials

Masking tape

Clock

Pencil sharpener

Stapler

Printed agenda

Participant names and addresses

Certificates of attendance

Throat lozenges

Add your own items to this checklist and eliminate those that aren't relevant to your presentation.

Appendix B

Titling Your Workshop

Coming up with a snappy, attention-getting title for your program can be time-consuming and frustrating. William C. Miller of Human Synergistics, Inc., in Plymouth, Michigan, provided a generic, off-the-shelf solution for readers of *Training*, a magazine for persons in the field of human resources development. Just pick one word from Column A, one from Column B, and one from Column C, in that order. Miller notes that this arrangement offers more than 17,000 combinations.[1]

COLUMN A	COLUMN B	COLUMN C
Achieving	Administrative	Abilities
Affirming	Basic	Attitudes
Appraising	Career	Awareness
Assessing	Crisis	Behavior
Building	Dynamic	Challenges
Centering	Employee	Change
Confirming	Executive	Climate
Coping	Group	Competence
Counseling	High-level	Comprehension
Creating	Human	Consensus
Dealing	Individual	Control
Developing	In-house	Decisions
Diagnosing	Intensive	Development
Enhancing	Interpersonal	Direction
Evaluating	Leadership	Education
Exploring	Management	Effectiveness

[1] Reprinted with permission from the July 1982 issue of *Training: The Magazine of Human Resources Development*. Copyright © 1982, Lakewood Publications, Minneapolis, MN, (612) 333-0471. All Rights Reserved.

COLUMN A	COLUMN B	COLUMN C
Facilitating	Mutual	Evaluation
Guaranteeing	Organizational	Feedback
Highlighting	Personal	Fulfillment
Implementing	Professional	Fundamentals
Increasing	Self	Goals
Influencing	Staff	Growth
Integrating	Strategic	Impact
Maintaining	Supervisory	Interaction
Motivating	System	Intervention
Negotiating	Team	Involvement
Planning	User	Learning
Providing		Models
Reaching		Needs
Remediating		Objectives
Rethinking		Performance
Revealing		Planning
Sharpening		Potential
Stimulating		Power
Strengthening		Practices
Uncovering		Principles
Understanding		Problems
Unlocking		Process
		Productivity
		Quality
		Relationships
		Research
		Resources
		Results
		Skills
		Standards
		Styles
		Synthesis
		Systems
		Techniques
		Theory
		Time
		Training
		Understanding

Appendix C

Workshop Evaluation

Your comments and suggestions can help improve this program. Please be as candid and specific as possible. Thanks for your help!

1. What is your overall reaction to this workshop? (Circle one)

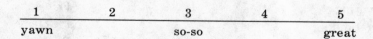

1	2	3	4	5
yawn		so-so		great

Comment:

2. Did the workshop meet your needs and expectations? Explain:

3. Which part(s) did you find most useful? Why?

4. Which part(s) did you find least useful? Why? Should they be shortened or eliminated?

5. On which topics would you prefer to spend more or less time?

6. Any further suggestions?

Appendix D

Detractor Detector

The best way to know how you're coming across to an audience is arranging to have yourself videotaped. If that's not possible, plant a friend in the audience and ask him or her to make notes on your general appearance, delivery, and content. This checklist suggests some things to look for:

EYES

_____ darted about aimlessly

_____ stared at the ceiling

_____ were riveted on your notes

_____ maintained good eye contact with the audience on all sides

HANDS

_____ fluttered like flags

_____ were invisible (locked behind your back or in your pockets)

_____ made smooth, fluid, meaningful gestures

FEET

_____ seemed glued to the podium floor

_____ paced like an expectant father

_____ rocked back and forth on your heels

_____ moved about easily but not restlessly

DELIVERY

_____ too loud

_____ too fast

_____ too rambling

_____ too slow

_____ too many, um, filler words, y'know?

_____ well paced and fluent

BODY LANGUAGE

_____ you slouched

_____ you stood stiff as a rooted tree

_____ you appeared relaxed and at ease

Finally, be aware of the unconscious habits that betray nervousness and attract more attention than the message you're trying to convey:

MANNERISMS

_____ ring twisting

_____ fiddling with other jewelry or tie

_____ lip licking or biting

_____ ear tugging

_____ pushing at the bridge of your eyeglasses

_____ drumming your fingers

_____ blowing hair out of your eyes

_____ tugging at jacket, skirt

_____ other: _____

Appendix E

Sample Press Release

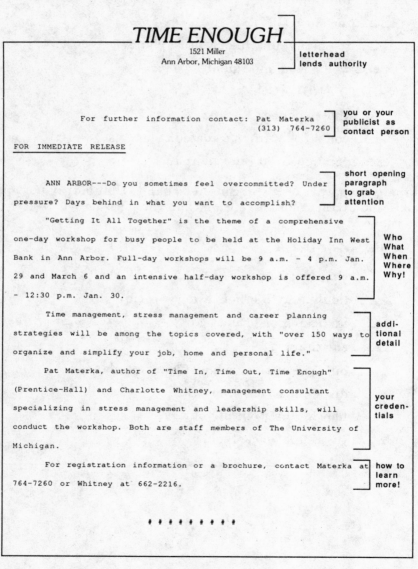

TIME ENOUGH

1521 Miller
Ann Arbor, Michigan 48103

letterhead
lends authority

For further information contact: Pat Materka
(313) 764-7260

you or your
publicist as
contact person

FOR IMMEDIATE RELEASE

ANN ARBOR---Do you sometimes feel overcommitted? Under pressure? Days behind in what you want to accomplish?

short opening
paragraph
to grab
attention

"Getting It All Together" is the theme of a comprehensive one-day workshop for busy people to be held at the Holiday Inn West Bank in Ann Arbor. Full-day workshops will be 9 a.m. - 4 p.m. Jan. 29 and March 6 and an intensive half-day workshop is offered 9 a.m. - 12:30 p.m. Jan. 30.

Who
What
When
Where
Why!

Time management, stress management and career planning strategies will be among the topics covered, with "over 150 ways to organize and simplify your job, home and personal life."

addi-
tional
detail

Pat Materka, author of "Time In, Time Out, Time Enough" (Prentice-Hall) and Charlotte Whitney, management consultant specializing in stress management and leadership skills, will conduct the workshop. Both are staff members of The University of Michigan.

your
creden-
tials

For registration information or a brochure, contact Materka at 764-7260 or Whitney at 662-2216.

how to
learn
more!

# # # # # # # # #

Appendix F

Sample Radio PSA

TIME ENOUGH

1521 Miller
Ann Arbor, Michigan 48103

Suggested Public Service Announcements For Use Through 28 January 1984

Anncr

(10 seconds)

(X) Learn to organize your life and avoid pressure through "Getting It All Together" workshops beginning January 29th in Ann Arbor.

For registration and cost information, call 764-7260 or 662-2216 during the day.

##########

Anncr

(30 seconds)

(X) Busy people <u>can</u> find ways to organize their professional and personal lives through time management, stress management, and career planning.

Attend "getting It All Together" workshops beginning January 29th in Ann Arbor.

The full-day and half-day sessions . . . taught by scholars of personal management and planning . . . will be at Holiday Inn West Bank.

For information on costs and to register . . . call 764-7260 or 662-2216 during the day.

##########

TIME ENOUGH presents . . .
A TIME MANAGEMENT WORKSHOP
for people with multiple responsibilities
at work and at home.

You will learn:

- Where the time "goes." How to use it more productively by setting priorities, planning ahead, establishing short- and long-range goals.

- How to spot and eliminate personal time-wasters such as clutter and paperwork, rambling meetings, unexpected visitors and phone calls.

- How to track your personal high energy "prime time" and preserve it for priority tasks. Sorting out high payoff activities from busywork.

- More effective ways to use lists, calendars, file systems, the telephone and other inexpensive, practical time manageement tools.

- Why overcommitment is good for you. Creating momentum, not stress. Delegation tactics that build cooperation, not resentment.

- How to organize anything: your desk, your work, your life. Creating an action environment in which you can find things fast and get things done.

- How to deal with indecision, worry, guilt and other time-draining hang-ups, including a five-step plan for overcoming procrastination — right now!

Specific topics include:

In your work life
- ☐ Uncluttering your desk
- ☐ Reducing paperwork
- ☐ Minimizing meeting time
- ☐ Delegating effectively
- ☐ Dealing with drop-ins
- ☐ Controlling phone calls

In your home life
- ☐ Reorganizing storage space
- ☐ Cleaning — quickly and rarely
- ☐ Cooking, shopping and laundry
- ☐ Entertaining made easy
- ☐ Errands, repairs, nuisances
- ☐ Sharing family chores

In your personal life
- ☐ Raising your energy quotient
- ☐ Stress management
- ☐ Getting away from it all
- ☐ Quality time with children
- ☐ What are friends for?
- ☐ Making your dreams a reality

Workshop Leader

Pat Materka is the author of *TIME ENOUGH*, a book offering a whole-life approach to time management, to be published in spring 1982 by Prentice-Hall.

She is a social sciences writer at the University of Michigan, teaches a course in time management and conducts workshops for individuals and organizations including business owners, homemakers, college faculty members, clerical workers and management personnel.

Past Participants Say . . .

"A very personal, practical approach to integrating daily tasks and responsibilities with long-range life goals."

"This workshop changed my life. In one week I reorganized half the house, updated my resume and delegated half of 'my' housework to my husband and children."

*"I came away feeling optimistic, motivated and buoyed with increased confidence that I **do** have control over my time and my life."*

What's in This for You?

- You'll develop a sense of "time consciousness"—a keen awareness of your personal priorities and how to take action on them.

- You'll learn to do less and accomplish more, by sharing hundreds of time-saving tips and strategies to simpify your life.

- In short—you'll know how to get done the things you *have* to do to make time for the things you *want* to do.

TIME ENOUGH   1521 Miller / Ann Arbor, Michigan 48103 / (313) 764-7260

BIBLIOGRAPHY

BOWER, SHARON ANTHONY. *Painless Public Speaking*. Englewood Cliffs, NJ: Prentice-Hall, Inc., 1981.

CARNEGIE, DALE. *The Quick and Easy Way to Effective Speaking*. Garden City, NY: Dale Carnegie and Associates, 1962.

COLLINS, KATHRYN S. *Marketing Noncredit Courses to Business and Industry*. Manhattan, KS: The Learning Resources Network, 1972.

CRAIG, ROBERT L. *Training and Development Handbook: A Guide to Human Resource Development*. New York: McGraw-Hill, 1976.

CROSS, K. PATRICIA. *Adults as Learners*. San Francisco: Jossey-Bass Publishers, 1981.

DAVIS, LARRY N. *Planning, Conducting and Evaluating Workshops*. Austin, TX: Learning Concepts, 1975.

DICKINSON, GARY. *Teaching Adults: A Handbook for Instructors*. Don Mills, Ontario: General Publishing Co. Ltd., 1973.

DRAVES, WILLIAM A. *How To Teach Adults*. Manhattan, KS: The Learning Resources Network, 1984.

FARLOW, HELEN. *Publicizing and Promoting Your Program*. New York: McGraw-Hill, 1977.

GOULD, J. SUTHERLAND. *How To Publicize Yourself, Your Family and Your Organization*. Englewood Cliffs, NJ: Prentice-Hall, Inc., 1983.

GROSS, RONALD. *The Lifelong Learner*. New York: Simon & Schuster, 1977.

GROSS, RONALD, ed. *Invitation to Lifelong Learning*. Chicago: Follett Publishing Co., 1982.

HODNETT, EDWARD. *Effective Presentations: How To Present Facts, Figures and Ideas Successfully*. West Nyack, NY: Parker Publishing, 1967.

KEMP, JERROLD E. *Planning and Producing Audiovisual Materials*. New York: Thomas Y. Crowell, 1975.

KNOWLES, MALCOLM. *The Adult Learner: A Neglected Species*. Chicago: Gulf Publishing Co., 1973.

KNOWLES, MALCOLM. *The Modern Practice of Adult Education*. Chicago: Follett Publishing Co., 1980.

MCKEACHIE, WILBERT J. *Teaching Tips: A Guidebook for the Beginning College Teacher*. Lexington, MA: D. C. Heath & Co., 1969.

MCLAGAN, PATRICIA A. *Helping Others Learn: Designing Programs for Adults*. Reading, MA: Addison-Wesley Publishing Co., 1978.

QUICK, JOHN. *A Short Book on the Subject of Speaking*. New York: McGraw-Hill, 1978.

SARNOFF, DOROTHY. *Make the Most of Your Best*. New York: Holt, Rinehart and Winston, 1970.

SHENSON, HOWARD L. *How To Create and Market a Successful Seminar or Workshop*. New York: Howard L. Shenson, 1981.

SIMMONS, S.H. *How To Be the Life of the Podium*. New York: AMACOM, 1982.

SMITH, TERRY C. *Making Successful Presentations: A Self-Teaching Guide*. New York: Wiley Press, 1984.

OTHER RESOURCES

The American Society for Training and Development (ASTD) is the national organization linking human resources personnel in business, industry, and education. Between 1972 and 1984, its membership more than tripled from 8853 to more than 28,000. For membership information, write:

> American Society for Training and Development
> Suite 300, 600 Maryland Ave., S.W.
> Washington, DC 20024

Periodicals of interest to trainers and adult educators include:

> *Training and Development Journal*, published by ASTD (address above)
>
> *Training: The Magazine of Human Resources Development* (731 Hennepin Ave., Minneapolis, MN 55403)

The Learning Resources Network (LERN), based in Manhattan, Kansas, serves as a national network for people and organizations providing adult and community education. It publishes two very useful periodicals: *Course Trends*, which tracks new and successful workshop and course topics in 15 subject areas; and *The Learning Connection*, containing "how to" articles on teaching adults, marketing, and other topics. For information on all of the organization's publications and services write:

> Learning Resources Network
> 1221 Thurston
> Manhattan, KS 66502

INDEX

academic institutions, 3
acoustics, 60–61
acting. *See* showmanship
adult education, 1–8. *See also*
    leaders, workshop
  demand for, 5–7, 27–28
  informality of, 10
  providers of, 2–5
  teachers of, 9–25
  unscrupulous and incompetent
    forms of, 7–8
adult learners. *See also*
    participants, workshop
  characteristics of, 28–31
  learning styles of, 31–33, 115
  motivating, 54–55
adult learning centers,
    independent, 4, 122–23
advertising, 128–29
alcoholism workshop, 79–80
Allen, Woody, 137–38
American Society for Training
    and Development (ASTD), 156
anatomy, 30
antagonists, 98
arguers, 98, 100–101
Associated Management Institute
    (AMI), 133–36
atmosphere, 60, 75–77
audience
  leader's knowledge of, 106–107
  questions of, 49–50
  rapport with, 94, 99

banquet-style seating, 62–64
Berlin, Lawrence S., 2–3, 7
blackboards, 65
body language, 117–18, 151
boredom, 92–94
brainstorming, 40, 77
breathing exercises, 109–111
brochures, 124–27
bull sessions, 40
Burpee, Robert L., 15, 88, 113–20
business and industry, 3
business cards, 26
buzz groups, 40

career-planning workshops, 42
careers
  changes in, 18
  new patterns of, 5
  promotion squeeze and, 6–7
catastrophes, 90–96
  prevention of, 94–96
census, U.S., 6
chalkboards, 65
Chamber of Commerce, 131
Ciampa, Diane L., 11–12, 69
classified ads, 129
classrooms, 62
closings, 78–80, 95
coffee breaks, 29, 30, 75
colleges and universities, 3
Collins, Carol, 108
Collins, Kathryn S., 125
comedy writing, 137–41

comfort, 61
"Community Leadership
    Development" (workshop),
    103–104
computers
    phobia of, 28–29
    technological change and, 5
conference tables, 62
consultants, 133–36
    fees of, 24
contacts, making, 17–18
continuing education. *See* adult
    education
Continuing Education Units
    (CEUs), 2
convenience, 60
Course Trends (magazine), 157
"Craft of Comedy Writing for
    Television, The" (workshop),
    21–22, 137–41
criticism
    constructive, 87–89
    sensitivity to, 15
cultural settings, 3–4
curiosity, 13

Davis, Frances, 129
Davis, Larry Nolan, 10
delivery, 116–19, 151
demonstrations, 40–41
design
    of brochures, 124–27
    of evaluation questionnaires,
        82–86, 148–49
    of visual aids, 67
    See also program design
detractor detector, 150–51
diad discussion format, 39
dignity, 29–30
direct mail, 92, 127–28
discussions
    facilitating, 46–51, 56–57
    importance of, 29
    lectures vs., 47, 57
    Osterman's method for, 56–57
    questions used in, 47–51
    tips for leaders of, 50–51
    types of, 39–40
Draves, William A., 1, 16, 76
"Dressing for a Professional
    Image" (workshop), 70

easels, 66

economic issues, courses and
    seminars on, 5–6
economics of workshops and
    seminars, 21–26
education. *See* adult education
educational attainment, 6
effective presentation of material,
    55
    See also program design
enthusiasm, 13
equipment, 35, 64–72
    catastrophe prevention and, 96
    handout materials, 72
    investing in, 96
    lecterns, 70
    microphones, 70–71
    name cards, 71
    name tags, 71
    props, 69–70, 77
    quizzes and questionnaires,
        71–72
    video, 69, 119
    visual aids, 64–69
evaluations, 81–89, 148–51
    negative, 87–88
    questionnaire design and,
        82–86, 148–49
    self-, 87
    testimonials, 88–89
    verbal, 86–87
exercises, 42
    breathing, 109–111
    stress reduction and, 109
expenses, start-up, 123–24
experience
    of adult learners, 28–29
    of workshop leaders, 11–12
eye contact, 118
eyes, use of, 150

facilities, 35, 59–61
Farber, Diane S., 18–19
feedback
    evaluations and, 81–89, 150–51
    on showmanship, 119–20
    verbal, 86–87
    written, 82–86, 148–49
feelers, 32–33
fees, 21–26, 92
feet, 117, 150–51
films, 68–69
filmstrips, 68
flannel boards, 66

flexibility, 14
flipcharts, 65, 66
freebies, 25–26, 131
"Freelance Writing for Glory and Profit" (workshop), 21
Fulkerson, Tavi, 70
full-group discussions, 40

games, 42
gestures, 117
goals, 34, 52–53

handout materials, 26, 72, 96
hands, use of, 117, 150
horseshoe seating arrangements, 62
hostility, 102–104
How to Organize and Manage a Seminar (Murray), 157–58
humor, sense of, 13–14, 79–80

icebreaker activities, 75–77
"in-basket" exercises, 42
independent adult learning centers, 4, 122–23
index card approach, 38
information
    gathering, 36–37
    selection of, 37–38
    sharing, 18

Johnson, Sandra, 23
Johnson, Spencer, 111
jokes
    insulting, 96
    See also humor, sense of
Jones, Charlie, 22
Jones, Kenneth W., 76, 88, 94, 117
Jung, Carl, 32

Kirby, Tess, 19–20, 88
knowledge of subject matter, 12–13
Kokkelenberg, Larry, 21, 133–36

language
    body, 117–18, 151
    sexist, 96
leaders, workshop, 9–25
    arrival time of, 73–74, 95
    boring, 92–94
    checklist for, 74, 144–45
    of discussions, 46–51, 56–57

inexperience of, 9–11
personal qualities and character traits of, 12–15
profit margins of, 21–24
psychic rewards of, 19–20
rewards of, 16–26
stage fright of, 105–12
visibility and contacts of, 17
learning
    climate for, 75–77
    readiness for, 54–55
    retention of, 55
    styles of, 31–33, 115
    See also adult learners
Learning Connection (magazine), 157
Learning Resources Network (LERN), 157
Learning Style Inventory, 32–33
lecterns, 70
"Lecture and Discussion Management" (seminar), 52–57
lecture halls, 62
lectures, 39
    discussions vs., 47, 57
Lemkuhl, Dorothy, 121
Liu, Christine, 121
lobby signs, 74
location, 35, 59–61
Loy, Lonnie L., 17

McCarthy, Bernice, 32
McClaran, Jeanne L., 105, 112, 119
mailing lists, 127–28
mannerisms, 151
Mapely, Faye, 13
marketing, 92, 121–32
    advertising, 128–29
    brochure design and, 124–27
    direct mail, 127–28
    press coverage, 129–30, 152
    radio stations and, 130, 153
    television stations and, 130–31
microphones, 70–71
Miller, William C., 146
monopolizers, 97, 100–101
motivation of adult learners, 5–7, 27–28, 54–55
Murray, Sheila L., 157–58

name cards and tags, 71
names, individual, 50

National Center for Education
    Statistics, 6
nervousness, 105–12
    positive vs. negative, 106
notebooks, personal, 87

observers, 101–102
opaque projectors, 67–68
openings, 73–77, 95
optimism, blind, 92
Osterman, Dean N., 32–33, 52, 99
overhead transparencies, 67–68
oversights, 94–95

pacing, 118–19
pads, newsprint, 65–66
Palmer, Barbara C., 158
Palmer, Kenneth R., 158
panic about speaking in public,
    109–10
participants, workshop. *See also*
    adult learners
    arguers, 100–101
    getting acquainted with, 75–77
    hostility of, 102–104
    involvement of, 52–57, 96
    marketing and, 131
    monopolizers, 97, 100–101
    problem, 97–104
    ramblers, 100–101
    side conversations of, 97–99
    silent, 97, 101–102
    types of, 34–35
Paul, Jeanne, 21, 61
pause, failure to, 118–19
performance. *See* showmanship
pitch, 118–19
population shifts, 6–7
positive self-talk, 110–12
posture, 117–18
presentation. *See* showmanship
press coverage and releases,
    129–30, 152
professional associations, 4
program design, 34–45
    audience characteristics and,
        34–35
    goals and, 34
    research for, 36–38
    teaching styles and, 38–42
    visual aids and, 64–69
projectors, overhead and opaque,
    67–68

promotion, 121–32
    self-, 123–32
    sponsors, 122–23
"promotion squeeze," 6–7
props, 69–70, 77
psychic rewards, 19–20
Public Service Announcements
    (PSAs), 130, 153
public-speaking panic, reduction
    of, 109–10

questionnaires, 71–72
    evaluation, 82–86, 148–49
questions
    brochures and, 125–26
    in discussions, 47–51
    evaluation, 82–86
    factual vs. open-ended, 48
    leading, 50
    short answers vs. open-ended,
        82–83
quirks, 119
quizzes, 71–72, 77

ramblers, 97, 100–101
radio, 130
rapport, 94
"reading" people, 50
recreation organizations, 4
Reed, John, 93–94
refreshments, 29, 75, 79
registration tables, 74–75
research, 36–38
    for discussions, 47
retention of what is learned, 55
role play, 41–42
room setup, 74
Rubenstein, Marla, 89

saboteurs, 104
Sarnoff, Dorothy, 105–106, 110
Scherger, Fran, 88–89
scripts, 42–45
seating arrangements, 61–64,
    95–96
    side conversations and, 99
self-confidence, 12–13, 110–12
self-deprecation, 108, 110
self-evaluation, 87
sexist language, 96
short-answer questions, 82–83
showmanship, 14–15, 113–20
    feedback on, 119–20

speaking style and, 116–19
side conversations, 97–99
silent participants, 97, 101–102
Sills, Beverly, 111
Simon, Danny, 21–22, 137–41
Simon, Neil, 138, 140
slides, 68
smoking, 29, 30
social organizations, 4
"Speaking as a Performing Art"
    (workshop), 113–14
speaking style, 116–19, 151
sponsorship, 122–23
Stafford, Colleen, 12, 103–104
stage fright, 105–12
    reduction of, 109–110
stamina, 15
Standard Rates and Data
    Service, 128–29
start-up expenses, 123–24
Steingold, Fred S., 17, 68, 88
stress, public-speaking, 109–110
stress management, 11–12, 69
*Successful Meeting Master Guide
    for Business and Professional
    People, The* (Palmer and
    Palmer), 158
Surgerer, Francine, 24

teachers
    requirements of, 9–15
    See also leaders, workshop
teaching
    rewards of, 16–26
    styles of, 38–42
    See also adult education
technological change, 5
television, 130–31
testimonials, 88–89
time consciousness
    of leaders, 73–74
    of participants, 30–31
    workshop design and, 35,
        58–59, 92, 93
time frame for discussions, 50–51
time management workshops, 95,
    122
    script for, 42–45
titles for workshops, 146–47

trade unions, 4
tranquilizers, 109
triad discussion format, 40
"trigger films," 42

"um" habit, 116
unemployment, 5–6

Van Voorhees, Curtis, 23, 25
verbal feedback, 86–87
videotapes, 68–69, 119
visual aids, 64–69
    design guidelines for, 67
voice, 118–20

women
    career patterns of, 5
    fair payment and, 24
    financial planning for, 18–19
    sexism and, 96
workshops and seminars
    catastrophes and, 90–96
    closing, 78–80, 95
    evaluation of. *See* evaluations
    fees for, 21–26, 92
    free, 25–26, 131
    free-flowing discussion in, 29
    goals of, 34, 52–53
    information sharing, 18
    Kokkelenberg on, 133–36
    leaders of. *See* leaders,
        workshop
    other resources on, 156–58
    participants in. *See* adult
        learners; participants,
        workshop
    parties compared to, 73
    promotion and marketing of,
        121–32
    researching and designing of,
        34–45
    Simon, Danny, on, 137–41
    site of, 35, 59–61
    size of, 139
    start of, 73–77, 95
    ten ways to insure success,
        142–43
    time of, 35, 58–59
    titles of, 146–47
    See also specific topics

Pat Roessle Materka has led hundreds of adult education workshops, lectures, and courses on time management and motivation, speaking before such organizations as Bechtel Corporation, the Maryland Center for Public Broadcasting, and the American Association of University Women. She has been a public information officer with the University of Michigan News and Information Services since 1971, has taught time management at Whitenaw Community College and the Ann Arbor Learning Network, and has published numerous articles for such periodicals as *Working Woman* and the *Detroit News*. She is the author of Prentice-Hall's *Time In, Time Out, Time Enough: A Time Management Guide for Women* (1982).